Thus Far on the Way:
Toward a Theology of Child Advocacy

Eileen W. Lindner

Louisville, Kentucky

First edition

Cover design and interior by Carol E. Johnson

Published by Witherspoon Press
Louisville, Kentucky

Web site address: www.pcusa.org/witherspoonpress

PRINTED IN THE UNITED STATES OF AMERICA

06 07 08 09 10 11 12 13 14 15 — 10 9 8 7 6 5 4 3 2 1

Library of Congress Cataloging-in-Publication Data

Lindner, Eileen W., 1949-
  Thus far on the way : toward a theology of child advocacy / by Eileen W. Lindner ; edited by Shannon Daley Harris. -- 1st ed.
    p. cm.
  ISBN 1-57153-058-4 (pbk. : alk. paper)
  1. Church work with children. 2. Child welfare. 3. Children's rights. I. Daley-Harris, Shannon. II. Title.
  BV639.C4L56 2006
  259'.22--dc22
                                          2006016264

To my own children, Andrew and Peter,

to all God's children, and to

the memory of Samuel DeWitt Proctor

Rev. Eileen W. Lindner is Deputy General Secretary for Research and Planning of the nation's largest ecumenical agency, comprising of thirty-six Protestant, Episcopal and Orthodox churches with a constituent membership exceeding 50 million North Americans. She is frequently asked to preach and teach around the country.

She is editor of the NCC's annual Yearbook of American and Canadian Churches, widely recognized as the most accurate and complete compilation of facts and figures on U.S. and Canadian churches and organizations.

She has previously served as Director of the Child Advocacy Office. She is the author of numerous books and articles on a variety of child advocacy subjects, most notably When Churches Mind the Children, reporting on the nation's most extensive child-care study.

Dr. Lindner is a member of the Good Schools Pennsylvania Founding Council and of the Steering Council for the Children's Defense Fund, Campaign to Leave No Child Behind. Rev. Lindner is a Presbyterian minister holding a Ph.D. degree in American Church History. She has served on national and international commissions dealing with topics related to children and to families. She serves as Theologian in Residence to the Children's Defense Fund's Summer Institute in Child Advocacy Ministry and as a member of the Board of Directors of Stand for Children.

Shannon Daley-Harris, editor of this book, served the Children's Defense Fund as Director of Religious Affairs for eight years, establishing the National Interfaith Observance of Children's Sabbaths and the Institute for Child Advocacy Ministry and authoring many publications, including the annual interfaith Children's Sabbath Manual, Holding Children in Prayer: An Advent Devotional, A Child Advocate's Concordance to the NRSV, and Welcome the Child: A Child Advocacy Guide for Churches (with Kathleen A. Guy). She now is a religious organizing consultant and writer for CDF and other organizations working on behalf of children and justice. She holds a B.A. in Religious Affairs, magna cum laude, from Brown University and an M.Div., summa cum laude, from Wesley Theological Seminary. Shannon is married to Sam Daley-Harris and is the mother of two children, Micah and Sophie.

Contents

Foreword

What does Jiffy Lube have to do with the prophets and the Gospel, or a grassy wading pool and glass of lemonade have to do with communion? To some, the combinations are as incongruous as a farm in Tennessee serving as the spiritual home and "seminary" of the children's movement. Yet once you have heard Eileen's Jiffy Lube and lemonade stories in the pages that follow, and once you have come to the Proctor Institute for Child Advocacy Ministry at the Children's Defense Fund's Haley Farm in Clinton, Tennessee, it will make the same sense as the last being first and the first being last, as the lion and lamb lying down together and a little child leading them. It will make as much sense as becoming as a child to enter God's realm, because to such as these the realm of God belongs.

In 1994, the Children's Defense Fund (CDF) bought the former Alex Haley Farm to be a center for spiritual renewal, character and leadership development, intergenerational mentoring, and interracial, interfaith, and interdisciplinary communication.

Just a year later, we hosted the first Institute for Child Advocacy Ministry during the third week of July. We wanted to create a week that modeled what we hoped all ministers and faith leaders would get in their preparation for ministry, what we wished every seminary provided, and how we hoped all churches would understand and live out their faith on behalf of children and justice.

I was eager to bring the prophetic voices of the nation's great preachers to preach on justice and children. We knew there was a need for solid, accurate information on children's concerns, which the CDF staff and others provide. We wanted to provide the skills and model programs through workshops so that participants could return to serve and speak out for children in their communities and help build a transforming movement for our children and nation in the early years of the twenty-first century. The remarkable glue that brought that first institute together, however, was the Reverend Dr. Samuel DeWitt Proctor (in whose memory the institute was renamed in 1997), who preached the morning devotions each day, and my dear friend Eileen Lindner, who led the theology and child advocacy sessions each morning as well as the closing communion at the week's end.

Eileen has the most remarkable capacity to use what she jokingly refers to as a long and very expensive education to communicate important and complex ideas in a way that is accessible not only to other PhDs but also to pastors with little formal education in ministry, lay leaders, and to everyone in between. Eileen's education has not been restricted to institutional learning, and she shares with us the lessons learned from children and church members, presidents and preachers, rabbis and refugees. The driving force behind it all is Eileen's passion for all of God's children and her passionate commitment to helping all who would be faithful to understand and live out our calling—as individuals and as a Church—to do justice, love mercy, and walk humbly with God.

The content of this book was not the solitary endeavor of a scholar hunkered down over her computer, but a conversation Eileen began eleven years ago with participants at the Proctor Institute through speeches, sermons, Bible studies, and communion services. It always amazes me to see Eileen head for the pulpit with no more than an index card or scrap of paper with just a few key words she has jotted down. From those brief reminders, Eileen goes on to unpack profound ideas, delve into biblical stories, and connect what it means in this day to be faithful to God's call to do justice for all our children. I hope that you will hear Eileen's voice in the following pages as the conversation continues.

The title of this book is drawn from a famous hymn by James Weldon Johnson, "Lift Every Voice and Sing." It recognizes that as faithful child advocates we are on a journey, a journey begun when the Hebrew midwives refused to kill the Jewish baby boys and baby Moses was kept from harm; a journey that continued as the wise men returned home by another way and Mary and Joseph fled to Egypt to protect baby Jesus. It is a journey that continued through the end of slavery and the civil rights movement and brought us to the edge of the Promised Land. Our journey has continued for more than thirty-five years as the Children's Defense Fund has worked in partnership with the religious community to ensure that we truly Leave No Child Behind and lead our children into the promised land of freedom and justice Dr. King foresaw. Most important, this book's title and the anthem for which it is named recognize that we have come thus far not by our own determination or efforts, but by God's might and grace—calling us onto this road and sustaining us along the way.

Over the eleven years of the Institute for Child Advocacy Ministry at CDF Haley Farm, Eileen's unforgettable stories, her warmth and pastoral sense, her quick wit and ready humor have not only made us laugh, opened our eyes, and touched our hearts but also forged individuals from all walks of life, all parts of the country, all races and ages and experiences into a community—a community that worships and learns and prays and acts and speaks out and stands together to bring God's love and justice to the children of our nation and world.

In the pages that follow, Eileen invites you into this community. Together, let us continue the journey to justice for all of God's children. By God's might and guidance, and with our hard work, we will come to the light of that day when all God's children can live the lives for which they were created.

In faith and hope,
Marian Wright Edelman
Founder and President
The Children's Defense Fund

Preface

The roots of all books, I suppose, are grounded in the seedbed of human experience. The sermons and theological reflections that follow are no exception. Raised in a decidedly Presbyterian home, my own early involvement with child advocacy took the form of serving as mentor and companion to my younger sister. Now a gracious and dignified middle-aged woman, she, then and now, ennobles the struggle with mental retardation and physical disabilities. For our family her nurture and assistance was a matter of love and faith. Ordained as a minister I came to recognize child advocacy as a justice ministry and a "calling" in the Calvinist understanding. Later still, as a mother to two beloved sons, Andrew Micah and Peter Martin, these commitments deepened even as their antics and insights clarified my theological understandings.

Yet, it was a chance encounter thirty-five years ago with Marian Wright Edelman, then Director of the Washington Research Project (that would soon become the Children's Defense Fund), that transformed my private calling into a public vocation. Through more than three decades of friendship I have admired Marian Edelman's leadership for children fired by her passionate faith, which has produced real and substantial gains for all our children. Heralded as a distinguished citizen servant, Marian would rather be heeded than heralded. She wears her myriad awards and honors lightly, preferring quiet reflection and prayer to adulation. I was therefore not surprised when she announced her intention to form a spiritual home for the children's movement and there unto summon all those who would stand for children in our society.

Since the founding of the Institute for Child Advocacy Ministry over a decade ago at the former Alex Haley Farm in Clinton, Tennessee, I have been privileged to join with mentor and friend Dr. Samuel DeWitt Proctor and later the distinguished Dr. Otis Moss Jr. and a host of others to minister among the remarkable and diverse souls who, like us, feel called to child advocacy and gather there for spiritual sustenance. Often in the course of preaching at the institute, brother Ron or another brother or sister would stand and call out "Talk!" The book that follows is drawn from those many presentations at Haley and is, in some ways, answering that call to "talk." It is a means to "talk" with other brothers and sisters who have not yet found their way "home" to Haley, offered in the hope it will be for you a sustaining word that resonates with your sense of calling to those children who are last, lost, and left behind.

These sermons and reflections were taped and transcribed and might have long languished in a forgotten desk drawer were it not for friends who encouraged and aided in their collection and publication. Marian's own urging that I publish them provided the initial encouragement and confidence that this could be another expression of the ministry of child advocacy. My dear friend the Reverend Jon Brown felt the project was a worthy one and introduced me to Sandra Albritton Moak, publisher with Bridge/Witherspoon Press. Her sound advice and ready enthusiasm made the prospect more plausible. Turning the project over to Martha S. Gilliss, editor with Bridge/Witherspoon Press, led to detailed planning for the project. To my delight, Martha assigned the editorial work on the project to my friend of long standing, Shannon Daley-Harris. Shannon is a consultant to the Children's Defense Fund and a notable child advocate in her own right who, during her tenure as CDF's Director of Religious Affairs, planned and directed the Institute for Child Advocacy Ministry for the first six years. Her careful work and wise recommendations allowed the volume to take shape. My gratitude to each of these companions in my journey of faith can scarcely be adequately expressed. I here thank each of them with a deep appreciation for the particular ways they have been friends to their colleague in ministry.

Thanks are owed, too, to the National Council of Churches of Christ in the U.S.A., which I have long served as staff, for the willingness to enable my participation each year at the Samuel DeWitt Proctor Institute for Child Advocacy Ministry at Haley Farm. Colleagues at the council have willingly made accommodation to my scheduling needs each July without hesitation or complaint. For this I am grateful for their recognition of and commitment to the justice ministry.

It is axiomatic but essential to acknowledge that despite being surrounded by this wonderful cloud of witnesses some errors may have stubbornly lingered. For such I bear sole responsibility.

To the warm, devoted, beautiful brothers and sisters who have attended the institute I wish to reserve my deepest thanks. No pastor could hope for a more faithful, passionate, or receptive congregation. Together we have sung, wept, prayed, rejoiced, and dismayed as we surveyed the mission field of child advocacy. Each year we have learned much from one another, sensed the presence of our God, renewed our commitment to the ministry of child advocacy, and have departed to serve. In some small measure I dare to hope that this volume will rekindle memories for those who have attended and will serve as an invitation to others to join us in coming home to Haley. Here then we recount some of the joy in the struggle as God has brought us *Thus Far on the Way*. May we always meet such abundant grace with grateful and joyful hearts.

Eileen W. Lindner
Epiphany 2006

CHAPTER ONE

Toward a Theology
of Child Advocacy

L ong ago I learned the importance of asking the right question.
Like most things that I have learned in life, I learned the importance of the right question through experience. I was at Washington National Airport on a snowy Friday just before Christmas. I was taking that aeronautical cattle drive known as the New York–Washington shuttle. It was the busy holiday season; of course, everybody was filled with Christmas cheer, pushing and shoving more than ever. It had been snowing—an unmitigated disaster in our southern capital city—and everyone was crowded into the cramped terminal. There's nothing quite like a few thousand people in a small space all smelling of wet wool.

I walked up to a very agitated airline ticket agent. I could see from a distance of thirty feet that she was in a terrible mood. When I got there, she barked, "Did anybody you don't know give you anything you don't know about?"

Now, I didn't want to provoke her, but I'm a person of the cloth. I have to answer truthfully. So, I said, "I don't know."

She knew trouble when she saw it coming. She stood there in her sturdy shoes and fixed me with her gimlet eye. She said, "I said that wrong. Do you have anything you don't know about from anybody you don't know?"

Oh, Lord. This is the improvement, huh? I had to say it. I had to say it. I said it again, "I don't know."

I saw her glance toward security. I knew whatever happened next would be my last chance to get home to my family for Christmas. She said, "Do you know what I'm trying to ask you?"

I said, "Yes, I think so."

"Did they?"

"No."

She said, "Here's your ticket."

It matters what question we ask! If ever we are to make sense of the answer, it matters profoundly what questions we ask.

In this book, I hope to outline a theological approach to child advocacy. That is, a theological discipline or framework that helps us better understand and live out our ministry of child advocacy. As we approach this task, it will indeed matter greatly what questions we ask.

I often find that the insights of other disciplines are useful to our own theological thinking. One such insight was shared with me by my youngest son, who serves as an Emergency Medical Technician (EMT) at our local volunteer ambulance corps. EMTs, as it turns out, learn many things that are helpful not only to emergency response but more generally to ministry.

One of the things EMTs learn is how to assess head trauma. With the proper assessment, when someone has been injured the extent of their injury and their symptoms can be quickly summarized. The EMT can then report to the doctor or nurse at the emergency room door that the patient is, for example, "alert and conscious, times four." Now, that doesn't mean much unless you know the lingo.

What it means to any medical person is that the patient is alert—that is awake and conscious. "Times four" means, in this order, that the person knows who they are, where they are, what time it is, and what just happened. These are four important orienting facets of human existence and EMTs quickly assess and report how their patients are doing in relation to these four questions.

In an accident, when someone suffers a head trauma, it's not unusual to forget what just happened. Maybe you've had this experience in a car accident or some other accident when you've hurt your head, or perhaps you know someone who did. That person would be described as "alert and conscious times three." That means they know who they are, where they are, what time it is, but they don't recall what just happened.

People who suffer in this way have retrograde amnesia. They've forgotten what just happened. If it's a more severe trauma they may forget what time it is, more severe yet, where they are. Identity is the last to go; in the most extreme case, they may forget who they are.

This offers us an interesting framework and metaphor for our theological reflection. I want to suggest that the goal of our striving is to be Christians, alert and conscious times four: to know who we are, where we are, what time it is, and what just happened. Such theological reflection is not, as often is supposed, the special province of scholars and theologians. Indeed the ability and responsibility to think theologically is one of the marks of the life of discipleship. Our theological reflections can and do help us to think afresh about the ways in which we are called to ministry and of its content. Other servants of God have, throughout time, struggled with the kinds of content represented by the EMT assessment of head trauma.

Moses: Alert and Conscious Times Four

Moses is an example of a fellow with a struggle to become alert and conscious times four. As we look at this story, ponder, will you, whether or not there's a story here about a theological discipline that helps us to ask ourselves to take a ready check and a ready assessment of our own hearts and minds each day. Do we know who we are, where we are, what time it is, and what just happened? Listen now for God's word to us in Exodus 3:1–15.

> Moses was keeping the flock of his father-in-law Jethro, the priest of Midian; he led the flock beyond the wilderness, and came to Horeb, the mountain of God. 2There the angel of the LORD appeared to him in a flame of fire out of a bush; he looked, and the bush was blazing, yet it was not consumed. 3Then Moses said, "I must turn aside and look at this great sight, and see why the bush is not burned up." 4When the LORD saw that he had turned aside to see, God called to him out of the bush, "Moses, Moses!" And Moses said, "Here I am." 5Then God said, "Come no closer! Remove the sandals from your feet, for the place on which you are standing is holy ground." 6God said further, "I am the God of your father, the God of Abraham, the God of Isaac, and the God of Jacob." And Moses hid his face, for he was afraid to look at God.

⁷Then the L ORD said, "I have observed the misery of my people who are in Egypt; I have heard their cry on account of their taskmasters. Indeed, I know their sufferings, ⁸and I have come down to deliver them from the Egyptians, and to bring them up out of that land to a good and broad land, a land flowing with milk and honey, to the country of the Canaanites, the Hittites, the Amorites, the Perizzites, the Hivites, and the Jebusites.

⁹The cry of the Israelites has now come to me; I have also seen how the Egyptians oppress them. ¹⁰So come, I will send you to Pharaoh to bring my people, the Israelites, out of Egypt."

¹¹But Moses said to God, "Who am I that I should go to Pharaoh, and bring the Israelites out of Egypt?" ¹²God said, "I will be with you; and this shall be the sign for you that it is I who sent you: when you have brought the people out of Egypt, you shall worship God on this mountain."

¹³But Moses said to God, "If I come to the Israelites and say to them, 'The God of your ancestors has sent me to you,' and they ask me, 'What is his name?' what shall I say to them?"

¹⁴God said to Moses, "I AM WHO I AM." He said further, "Thus you shall say to the Israelites, 'I AM has sent me to you.'" ¹⁵God also said to Moses, "Thus you shall say to the Israelites, 'The L ORD, the God of your ancestors, the God of Abraham, the God of Isaac, and the God of Jacob, has sent me to you': This is my name forever, and this my title for all generations."

Well, is Moses alert and conscious times four? Let's have a look.

Who Are You, and Whose Are You?

Who are you? How central this question is. Remember that identity is the last thing to go. It's only gone when the head injury is very severe. Our identity is more than just our name, it is our sense of ourselves.

Perhaps it is for this reason that the Church marks this in its ordinance or practice of christening. Here is your name. Here, little child, is what you shall be called. This is the word we will say when we mean you.

Now, I grew up in a big family. And one of the great benefits— not that I was ever doing anything wrong, mind you, but sometimes people thought I might be—and one of the blessings of a large family is that Grandma has to work her way through about twelve names before she gets to you. That gives you an opportunity to correct your behavior before she gets to the right name.

But our name is so much a part of us. Who are you? I'm Jane. Who are you? I'm Mark. Who are you? I'm Vincent. Who are you? I'm Moses. The Church recognizes the center of identity. We are often named for someone whom our parents admire, whose finest qualities they hope will be reflected in their child.

But knowing that name, knowing who you are, doesn't answer the question completely. For Moses and for us, the answer to the question, Who are you, do you know who you are? is inextricably bound up with the question, Do you know *whose* you are?

Who are you, whose are you? You do not belong to yourself. You do not belong even to this company of people who love you. But you belong to your creator.

Whose you are sets the stage for who you may become. Look at Moses. Moses has more than enough reason to be confused about his identity, doesn't he? So, who are your parents, Moses? Where did you grow up? What was your hometown?

Well, it was a basket of reeds. My family was, well my mother was . . . well, I had family, sort of. Where do you live, what's your hometown? Well, it's Egypt, but that's not really where I am from.

Moses had no clue, did he, who he was? He didn't know his parents, he didn't know his hometown. I mean, talk about having no zip code; he couldn't even call the name of his town. His parentage had been confused in one of the great conspiratorial epics of human history, so he couldn't give us his family chart.

He didn't know who he was, but he came to know *whose* he was. And maybe to be alert and conscious times one, we don't need the details of our CVs, our résumés, or our titles. We only have to know whose we are. To whom do we belong? The one who made you, who knew you before you were born, who knit you together, who placed you on this earth. To be alert and conscious times one is to know *whose* you are.

And therein lies the beginning point of theological discernment. Who am I, whose am I, and who is that God who created me? When we can answer with assurance, we are alert and conscious times one.

Where Are You? Here I Am, Send Me

If we are to be more fully alert in our life and witness we will need also to ask where we are. Where are you? Do you know where you are? For many of us it means, do you know your location? You know, they have these little GPS devices in cars now to tell you where you are on the face of the entire globe. Now, I don't have one of those devices. And I have been said to be geographically and directionally challenged. But I can't think what help it would be to me to know the longitude and latitude of where I am. I don't want to know latitude and longitude; I want a contextual description of where I am.

Do you know where you are? Well, Moses had a little trouble with that question. Where am I? God said, "You are on holy ground." I suggest that whenever you are in the presence of your God, you are on holy ground. At any longitude or latitude, you can be on holy ground. When you know whose you are and you stand in God's presence, you are on holy ground. That's where you are.

Remember whose you are, remember that you stand in the presence of your God, and answer, "Here I am." Where am I? I'm right here. O God, I'm right here in your presence. Ripe for the sending. Alert and conscious times two. We know whose we are, we know where we are, and we can respond, here I am, send me, to serve the God to whom we belong.

What Time Is It? The Hour of Freedom

A harder question is, do we know what time it is? Now, one of the delights of traveling is you get to change time zones. If you're very fortunate, you even get to cross the dateline, which allows you to get some place before you left. It is an exciting travel experience but it does demonstrate the disconcerting effect travel has on our sense of time. Timeliness, of course, is determined by factors quite unrelated to clocks or timekeeping.

When I think about what time it is, I think of my experiences of world travel. I think of the mothers in Chile. These are women who daily go to the plaza to remind their countrymen and their government that they are still wondering about their sons and some daughters who have disappeared. As the women walk in a circle carrying the photographs of their missing children someone will cry out ¿*Qué hora es?* What time is it? ¿*Qué hora es?* literally, What hour is it?

The answer called out in response is, *Esta es la hora de la libertad.* It is the hour of freedom.

¿*Qué hora es? Esta es la hora de la libertad.* What time is it? It is the hour of freedom. ¿*Qué hora es? Esta es la hora para la libertad,* it is the hour for freedom. The answers aren't so very hard after all.

For Moses the question of the time was relatively clear. He may have been reluctant to lead but he knew for certain that the moment had come for the Israelites to seek their freedom. The moment had come for the people to leave the life of servitude and indignity they had so long known and set out for a distant promised land they had not seen but to which God called them.

To be alert and conscious times three is to know whose you are, where you are, and what time it is. I am God's, I'm here and ready to be sent, and it's the hour for freedom.

What time is it for you? What season of your life is this? Is it the season of hope when all things are possible? The season when you look and think what shall I be, where shall I go, where do I make my contribution? Or is this the season of autumn or even winter, when you're tempted to live and dwell in your regrets and to refuse God's answer, *Esta es la hora de la libertad,* it is the hour of freedom. In the winter or spring of your life, it is the hour for freedom as it is in all the hours in between. *Esta es la hora para la libertad.* It is the hour for freedom.

Whose are we, where are we, what time is it? Who are you? Whose are you? Where are you? Where are you on your faith journey? What time is it?

What Just Happened?

Now, the really hard question: what just happened? I suggest that one of the reasons we so seldom know what just happened is that we have spent a lifetime misleading people about what just happened.

Where does this bad practice start? I think it starts when you are a child and you accidentally (or accidentally on purpose) break something with a great crash. Your mother yells from another room, what's going on?

Your answer? Nothing! What's going on up there? Nothing!

Why is it we don't know what just happened? We have spent the whole of our lives misleading one another about what just happened.

I had a very wily mother. Some say it's because she had wily children. After a time, about the trouble years, which are, you know, more or less immediately after birth onward, she stopped asking what just happened, because she knew what the answer was.

And I would run to her, "Mom, Mom, Terry (my older brother) just hit me." She never asked, what did you do? Because the answer to that is . . . nothing!

She always asked, "Eileen, what happened just before he hit you?"

Now, I didn't realize I was being drawn in. So, I would say things like, "Well, you know, I don't know. He was building that model plane and I just stepped right near it. And its wing fell off."

What just happened? How often do you find yourself stunned? What just happened? Years ago, many of us had brave hopes for what would happen. We thought we had elected a president who had access to good information about children and their needs, families and their needs. Oh, we had so hoped. Oh, we looked forward to a policy that would reform welfare.

And then the one in whom we had lodged such hope signed a bill that told a lie, that said it was about welfare reform when it was about welfare meanness, when it was about denial, and didn't we shake our heads and say, my Lord, what just happened? What just happened here?

After that disappointment of welfare reform, which we had hoped would improve the lives of children and didn't, many of us in the child advocacy movement rallied and, with the Children's Defense Fund's leadership, committed ourselves to a campaign to Leave No Child Behind. This time, we felt, we had staked out our ground in public policy and had unequivocally expressed our concern for all children. This time, we thought, we cannot be thwarted or disappointed. Sadly, it was only a few months later when another president brought to bear an educational effort that penalizes the very children who need help. And the indignity of it all is that he hijacked the phrase, twisted into No Child Left Behind, as the sound-good smoke screen behind which money for poor children was again reduced.

Do you know what just happened? What just happened? is an indispensable question for child advocates and for all Christians who would be faithful.

For a very long time many in the black community have asked the question, what just happened? about children being gunned down. But too many white brothers and sisters turned a blind eye until Columbine opened their eyes and only then did they say, my God, what just happened?

I recall a segment on the *Today Show*. They had what in this day of electronic media is a long and thorough story; it took five or six minutes. You know, they really wanted to get to the bottom of all this. They were doing a story about a white gangsta rap artist—let's say singer. "Oh," they said, "this is terrible, these lyrics are terrible."

And they interviewed parents in those great big vehicles dropping their children off at this white gangsta rap concert or whatever one calls such events. They asked one mother, "Madam, have you ever listened to this man's lyrics?"

"No," she said, "but the children love him." Oh, swell. What day is she going to ask what just happened? When is she going to say, what just happened here?

When are we as a culture going to say, what happened here? What just happened here? What happened between the proud words "that all men are created equal, that they are endowed by their Creator with certain unalienable Rights" and the history of slavery? What just happened? What happened between "I have come to proclaim release to the captives" and our nation and world today? What happened between the time it was said, "Let them have life and that abundantly," and the decision to fund less than half of the poor and disabled infants and preschoolers who are eligible for Head Start?

What just happened? It's hard to say. It's hard to know what just happened, and we start to develop retrograde amnesia. We don't know what just happened. We don't want to know what just happened.

I suggest to you the primary theological task of our generation is to ask ourselves what just happened, what has happened among us? What has happened to our culture, what has happened to the promise given in documents sacred and secular? What happened to the promise that we should look upon each other's face and see not race or class or clan or age, but look into each face and see the image of God for God made them in God's own image?

Well, this then is our theological construct. Can we adapt the EMT's questions to our theological ends? Can we ask ourselves who are we, where are we, what time is it, and what just happened? Maybe our answers will not be unlike Moses'.

How close do our answers come to Moses'? Who are you? Well, the question is, whose am I? And for Moses the answer was, "I'm the child of the God who already knows my sufferings, who says, 'I know, I have observed the misery of my people.'" We are those who belong to the God who already knows, who knows about Head Start, who knows about welfare reform, who knows that public education is walking around with a bull's eye over its heart and another one around the back of its head. That's whose we are.

Where are we? We're on holy ground. We're on holy ground, because God is here. So, let us take off our sandals, let us feel that earth more closely. Where are we? We are on holy ground. Now, Moses is a little slow to get that thoroughly in his mind, so he just resolves it by saying, here I am. When God talks to you, will you do as well, will you say, here I am? Here I am standing on holy ground remembering that I'm yours.

What time is it? Well, that's the hard one. There is an Internet site designed for preachers who are running out of time to get their sermons written. On Saturday—I have been told—the Web site opens a chat room at noon East Coast time, and it continues until 3 A.M. Pacific time. Those West Coast brothers and sisters have to preach, too. It's an opportunity for those who are running a little behind schedule to discuss together, in a chat room, the lectionary— the assigned text for the week. To share insights and to share a sense of desperation about what time it is.

What time is it? Are you in a hurry? Should you go faster or should you go slower? It all has to do with what time you reckon it to be. We so often let the hour on our watch or the date on our birth-day calendar or the hour and day and month of the year determine what we think we can do. Can't do that now, the legislature's out of session. Can't tend to that now, the church bazaar is next week. Can't be bothering with the homeless when the church bazaar is coming up. Can't do that now, I'm forty-five. Could have done it when I was twenty-five, but can't do it now. Can't do it now, I'm only twenty-two. When I get older.

What time is it? When the question is asked in relation to some important effort in child advocacy, maybe your heart will sing back to you, *esta es la hora para la libertad*. It is the hour for freedom, for action, for service, for advocacy.

Well, Moses wasn't plagued with the time question. But we have that very strange line when God spoke out of the bush, "Moses hid his face." I guess it wasn't time to face God.

God speaks out of the burning bush of your city, your children and your families, your parish, of this nation and our world. Nearly thirteen million American children are living in poverty. Twenty-nine percent of the children alive today in sub-Saharan Africa will die before they're five years old. What time is it? *Esta es la hora para la libertad*. It must be the hour for freedom for those children. When God speaks to you, will you hide your face or will it be the hour in which you face God, face to face, saying, "Here I am, send me."

I remember being a young teen when I heard John F. Kennedy say, "Ask not what your country can do for you; ask what you can do for your country" (Inaugural address, 1961). And I thought I had never heard more musical words. As I look back on it, I think they spoke to my heart for two reasons. One, because it was an important man calling me, Eileen Williams. He was right there on my television, talking directly to me. Oh, I know there were others listening in, but right to me. Do something important with your life, that's what he said.

President Kennedy said something else. He said something to us that we have stopped saying to our children: you have something to contribute to this nation. We, on the other hand, have implied to our young people and our children: you are potential and you might someday be worth something, but you have nothing to contribute now. John Kennedy said you have something to give. Ask yourself what it is. What time is it? It's the time to ask these questions.

What just happened? Well, in Moses' story what just happened is something else again. Moses knows he has to go down that mountain with some kind of story about bushes burning, not being consumed, God's talking, telling him names, telling him about pharaoh, the worst problem that his people have ever encountered.

Well, something did just happen. I don't know what just happened for you, but something happened to put you on the path to child advocacy. Something happened that spoke to your heart. Something as crazy as a bush burning without being consumed happened to bring you to a place in your life that you are asking theological questions about child advocacy. Something as nutty as God saying take your sandals off, you're on holy ground. Something as nutty as God speaking into your heart and saying, you know, that pharaoh, it doesn't have to be. You could get on with it and it doesn't have to be.

Alert and conscious times four. Let us accept the theological discipline to ask ourselves who are we, where are we, what time is it, and what just happened. Then let us amend that last question, change that "j," to ask not what *just* happened but what *must* happen. And then find our own sure answer.

As we ask these questions, we will start by looking at traditional Christian doctrine and at Scripture to answer the question who and whose we are. Then we will turn to a theology of leadership and missiology to answer the question of where we are, to discern what it means in this day to answer, here I am, send me. To answer the question of what time is it, we look to the historical witness of the church: How has the church over the ages understood its calling, its responsibility, its mission? How has it understood the place of children in the life of the church? It is indeed the hour for freedom, and so we will explore the concept of the Church as a sanctuary for children. Finally, we look at what just happened, the context, and seek to discern what the Holy Spirit calls us to do, to say, and to be in this moment. James Russell Lowell, in one of his great hymns, says, "New occasions teach new duties. Time makes ancient good – uncouth." And so in every situation, every situation in life, every context, we must ask again, what is faithful? What is true? What does the Holy Spirit call us to in imitation of Jesus? Christian folk of every age have tried to remain faithful to their calling by repairing to Scripture, the historical witness of the church, and the contemporary stirring of the Holy Spirit in discerning what is true and right for their respective generations. Today we, too, take up that task as we move toward a theology of child advocacy.

CHAPTER TWO

Who and Whose Are We?

Nine Doctrines for a Theology of Child Advocacy

Borrowing the head trauma assessment questions from the medical profession, we want to pursue further our exploration of the theology that informs our ministry as child advocates. Can questions formulated for assessment of injury serve us well in our understanding of the demands of faithfulness today? We believe they can, and the first question we seek to answer with greater depth and detail is *Who and whose are we?* Today, we look at the question of theology: toward a theology of child advocacy.

In this chapter we want to examine nine constructs or doctrines that may speak particularly to the ministry of child advocacy. These are various beliefs people of faith have developed through their reading of the Bible, the lived experience of faith, and the inspiration of the Holy Spirit. Each, I believe, informs the faithful ministry of child advocacy.

The Image of God

Many of our Christian doctrines of origin come from ancient near-Eastern cultural practice and/or the tradition of the Hebrew scripture and the tradition of Judaism. The first of these doctrines is the image of God. What does that have to do with child advocacy? According to Hebrew scripture, God says explicitly in Genesis and implicitly throughout the rest of Hebrew Scriptures that every face is an icon, an image, a copy of the face of God. Each one is created in the image of God. We see in the newborn baby not just a child who favors his mommy or his daddy, because whomever he favors in kinship, each child favors the Everlasting God. That is for whom we advocate: those who are shaped and formed in God's own image.

Child advocacy is in and of itself a rather seductive problem for the Church. How many of us have pictures of our children in a wallet, a bag, or a briefcase, including those children who are now fifty-two years old? We love our own children, but we do not always love children or childhood in general. In fact, as a nation and even as a Church we're rather hostile to children. And, if not hostile then at least indifferent to the millions of children globally who are poor, hungry, sick, and without education. We know there are children languishing in poor facilities, homeless on our streets, or confined to various forms of prison largely because they have no responsible adult in their lives. But we let ourselves off the hook, remain indifferent, because we tend, especially in America, to see children as the private property of their parents.

As Christians it's time we make a commitment to those photographs that are in God's wallet. Imagine what a billfold that is, one of those accordion things that unfold to reveal all of the pictures. Imagine taking the end of God's billfold pictures and running to the ends of the earth until it is unfurled, encircling the globe. Let's think about God's wallet. Let's honor all of those children.

One of my friends is a Greek Orthodox priest who was a medic in Vietnam, drafted right out of high school. He became a corpsman, a kind of first aid person. So, he was in Vietnam with responsibility for treating young men, young soldiers, who had been injured or wounded by gunfire or burnt by napalm.

He says of this experience, "It was only in bandaging the faces of those burned with napalm that I came to understand what a holy vocation iconography is: to put back the face of Christ."

Do we have to wait until they are burned by napalm? Can't we see Jesus in the face of every child? Can't we see the Lord of life in each of God's children?

The Orthodox, and other Christians who use icons, venerate and honor those icons. Do we honor icons of Christ who are born too small, too early, too poor, without enough care? No, we dismiss them. We dismiss them unless they are children of our own hearts. So, the first doctrine to reclaim in this theology of child advocacy is the notion of the imago Dei. That is, we need to restore and strengthen our perception of children as being created in the image of God.

Doctrine of Justice

The second theological tradition we inherit from Hebrew Scriptures is the doctrine of justice. From the eighth-century prophets, we hear the call to justice in many expressions and in many ways. But it is summed up, I think perhaps most precisely, in Micah 6:8b, "And what does the LORD require of you? That you live justly, love tenderly [or, love kindness] and walk humbly with your God.

You know, we keep getting confused on this point, don't we? Remember in that context the prophet says, 6"With what shall I come before the LORD." I know, it's rivers of oil. That's what you want, right? Burnt offerings. No, no, perhaps it's my first-born.

The Lord responds, Old man, what is wrong with you? Not oil or offerings or first-borns but this: that you live justly, that you love tenderly, that you walk humbly with your God.

When I was ordained some thirty years ago very few women were ordained in the Presbyterian Church. The pulpit robe company didn't make women's pulpit robes so my home church had a robe made for me. Anyway, it was Christmastime. I wore my fancy robe. I know it's going to be hard to believe, but I was rather full of myself. It was an Advent service and we had an Advent wreath. I called a young girl to light the candles on the Advent wreath, and I did what all pastors do. I gave her exceedingly exact directions. I said to her, "When the time comes, I'll nod. You come down, light the candle, then turn, blow out the match without blowing out the candle, and go sit down." Implicit in my directions was that I, of course, would come and do the important stuff. (You see it coming, don't you?)

I nodded, she came up, did exactly as I told her, and as I moved over to the Advent wreath, she said in very clear voice, "Careful, Reverend, don't set your bathrobe on fire."

You know, I've thought over the years, "Reverend, don't set your bathrobe on fire" is a rather good charge for a new minister. But I don't feel right in that charge unless they add, "But you ought to smell it singeing a time or two. You ought to see a little whiff of smoke pass by your eyes. Don't set it right on fire. But let it smolder a little bit, because you're nudged up pretty close to the flame."

Because if you're not, you're not doing right. So surrounded as we are by so great a cloud of witnesses, let us be flirting with that flame. Don't set our bathrobes on fire, but come very, very, very close, let us have a little smell of singed material wherever we pass, and we will be on the right end of the love–justice continuum.

The Reverend Bill Coffin would always say institutions cannot love. But the corporate [not as in big business, but as in what we do as a body, together] expression of love is justice. So, our missiological intent is this: that in our personal interactions love will mark us as the children of Christ, and we will refuse to live in a society that does not promote justice.

Robert Kennedy used to say that the arc of history is long, but that it bends toward justice. I'm not seeing much bend. I'm hearing some justice rhetoric and it's a confusing thing, you know. I hear a lot of justice rhetoric, but I'm not seeing that arc curve toward anything that looks like justice to me.

The church needs to find its voice and it needs to find its voice fast. Our children are hungry, they're in poor health, and I think particularly of the young black men in prison. Let us not pretend that the young can't change, let us not pretend that good folks don't come out of prison. Paul came out of prison, didn't he? Then there was that fellow who was in a Birmingham jail. Then there was Nelson Mandela and then there was that one, jailed, tried, and taken to a cross. And then He redeemed the world. We must prevent so many young people, especially young black men, from winding up in prison. It is not good for their health, it is not good for their souls, and it is not good for our society. Why is it that we as a nation can guarantee a child a jail cell, but we can't guarantee them health insurance or three square meals or a roof over their heads on the outside? We have to set them free, get them home, and most important, do all that we can and must to end the cradle-to-prison pipeline that seems to prepare far too many children, Jesse Jackson notes, from birth on a path to jail while only a select few are set on the path to Yale.

Doctrine of Mercy

Related to this doctrine of justice is the doctrine of mercy and it is as essential as the doctrine of justice to a theology of child advocacy.

The first year I was ordained, I was studying at the University of Chicago and was an associate pastor at a suburban church. The pastor went on vacation in August, leaving me alone with this church of 1,200 members, when I'd been ordained all of about two months. He was a man of faith, needless to say. Fortunately, most of the congregation was also on vacation, so I couldn't do too much wrong.

One day I received a terrible phone call. There was a family in church who had tried to have children for many long years and had many miscarriages. They had finally given birth to a daughter and had raised her in the church. She had just graduated high school in June.

These were now the end days of August, and they took her off to college, only a few hours away, to be enrolled as a freshman. And when they returned home, they had a terrible phone call that she had been killed in an automobile accident. It was an accident, not carelessness, no drunk driving, no negligence, no speeding, just two young people colliding on a street corner and their daughter was gone. Killed in a traffic accident on her very first day at the university.

Kin to the family called the church, and I shakily made my way over. Nothing in seminary quite prepares you for this moment, and I was concerned about what I would say. I was focused on the wrong thing, of course. I made my way up the walk and knocked on the door, knowing the woman who answered the door would have her heart broken. She opened the door and I could see the wreckage of that broken heart in her face.

She invited me in and I quickly looked around for her husband. I asked, "Where is Walter?" "Oh," she said sadly, "Walter's gone to find the boy." Oh, my Lord, be with me, I thought, he's gone after the boy.

I said, "He's going after the boy? He's gone to find the boy? The driver of the other car?"

"Yes," she said.

I asked, "What's he going to do?"

She responded, "Well, this is terrible you know. We've lost our daughter. We've lost Carolyn. But we cannot lose two young people over this. Walter's gone to find the boy to tell him it's all right. That we can't lose two young lives over this."

I must confess to you now, after more than thirty years of ministry, I have found more than once that I arrive at the house or the hospital bed or the workplace or some other spot not to instruct but to be instructed by the witness of those who know what it means to temper justice with mercy. Who know what it means to live justly, to love tenderly, and to walk humbly with their God.

If we fail to love mercy, and if we misunderstand justice as vengeance, then we will fail to see the way ahead in this faithful journey of child advocacy. A rabbi friend once told me a wonderful rabbinic story.

A man did an exceedingly good deed and the angel of the Lord came to the man, and said, "You may have three wishes, any three wishes you like. But the Lord of the universe is saddened that you have an enmity, a fight with another. So, whatever you select for yourself will be given to you. But that very thing *twofold* will be given to your enemy." Then the angel departed for a few days to give the man time to ponder.

So, the man thought and thought. Perhaps, he thought, I'll have me a bag of gold. Then he thought, well, wait, my enemy will get two bags. Well, maybe I'll have a farm, many head of cattle. No, no, that won't do. My enemy would then have a farm twice as big as mine with twice as many cattle. Then he thought, maybe I'll have sons. And on and on his pondering went.

Finally the day arrived and the angel came to him. Still the man couldn't decide. He was stuck, you know. He was stuck between grace and enmity, he couldn't let go of that enmity to seize the grace, the mercy.

He waited, he waited, and he waited, and he thought of all the wonderful things he and his family might enjoy, but in the end he just hated the other too much.

The angel said to him, "The time is now, what will you have?" And with a broken heart the man answered, "Make me blind in one eye. Make me blind in one eye. Let my enemy be thrown into darkness and despair. This I will choose instead of choosing the way of grace."

In contrast, think of Nelson Mandela. He walked out of a prison and into a presidency and he didn't say, as is the custom, Bring my enemies to me that I might shoot them. He walked out of a prison. He walked into a presidency and, God love him, he invited his tormentors to share with him in the governance of a free South Africa. Out of a prison and into a presidency and he said, Come, come, my tormentors, my jailers, come. And let us together find a new way. Let us together find the South Africa that ought to be. Men who walk from prisons to presidencies remind us of what it means to temper justice with mercy.

Unlike Nelson Mandela, for the most part we seem so unable to choose the way of mercy that will bring the greatest blessing to those children and families that we deem unworthy or unlovable or undeserving. And in failing to choose the way that will bless them most, our nation is blinding itself and losing its way.

The Peaceable Kingdom

The fourth great construct we receive from the Hebrew tradition is the intent for the restoration of a Peaceable Kingdom. We'll see later in the Gospel of John that in many ways this concept, this ancient concept of a cosmos in harmony with itself and its Creator, is expressed in the concept of *koinonia* and the beloved community. But here in Hebrew Scripture we first glean that God has created us for life together so that we live in harmony with one another and with all living things.

Now, I've never lived more than an hour from a major city in all my life. So, I never gave much thought to the birds of the air or the fish in the sea until I had two sons. You have no idea what a brisk trade I've done in animal funerals since I started raising sons. I have buried frogs and goldfish. Then there was Cookie the hamster and dogs and cats. And so enthusiastic were my children that they lent me out for funerals in the neighborhood to other children who had suffered a loss in the passing of their pets. Ours is a very diverse community, and I learned to pray the Kaddish for Jewish pets. We had many an interfaith service.

There was a time when one of my children was in nursery school and they called me one day, saying "Reverend Lindner, you had better come here quick. Peter is upset. We can't get him to stop crying."

I said, "That's all right. I'll be right there." Twelve minutes, the Lord was with me and the NYPD was not, and I got to the nursery school. My son was sobbing. You know, when children weep there is nothing like it—big red eyes, tears all over the tee shirt, nose running, that kind of cry. This was clearly a full-blown crisis. I asked the teacher, "What happened?"

She explained, "We had a fire drill. We told the children to go to George Street," the little quiet street on the side of the nursery school.

The children knew the fire drill instructions. Get in line, go with their partners, follow the teachers, go to George Street. Go to George Street, children. If you get lost from one another, go to George Street. If you get mixed up, turned around, confused, where are you going to go? If you're hurt and lost and you don't know where anybody is, where are you going to go? George Street. Sounds pretty good to me.

I turned to Peter, "What happened?"

He said, "Cookie."

"Cookie. Who is Cookie?" I asked.

"Our hamster," he snuffled.

"Where is Cookie?"

"I didn't want her to burn. I opened her cage. I told her to go to George Street."

Now, of course, Cookie was lost and my poor sobbing son spent the afternoon walking around looking for this hamster, and I have to tell you, I don't know if I was rooting to find her or not find her. If I found her, I was afraid I was going to have to pick her up.

He said you're hurt or lost, go to George Street. If they took away Head Start, go to George Street. If they took your daddy's job, go to George Street. Well, where in the "hmm" is George Street? We have told one another in this land of ours that there would be a George Street.

I should fill you in on Cookie. That night, of course, no one could have dinner at the Lindner home. So we gathered a few neighbors, and we all went to George Street and the Methodist Church and we looked for Cookie. Well, there was no hope for it. That next Friday night, we were having dinner when the phone rang. It was the reverend down at the Methodist Church where the nursery school is. That pastor was having a wedding rehearsal, and when the organist hit that old four-one chord for Purcell's trumpet voluntary, Cookie headed for George Street. Snagged by a member of the wedding party who was fleet of foot.

Where is George Street? Where is George Street? The last, the least, the lost, and the little need George Street. Can you point us the way? Do you know where it has gone?

There's something to be learned about the cosmos from small children with their love for pets. One might ask, on behalf of both the children and the pets in harm's way, where is George Street in our society today, where the vulnerable might repair and be safe? Where is the hope of a Peaceable Kingdom in our war-weary world?

So, these are the four great doctrines from Hebrew scripture: *imago Dei*, the doctrine of justice, the doctrine of mercy, and the Peaceable Kingdom. Let's turn now to uniquely Christian doctrine.

Doctrine of the Incarnation

The fifth doctrine for a theology of child advocacy is the whole notion of incarnation. What a concept. Now, we take for granted the doctrine of the incarnation. We remember the birth story, the birth narrative of Jesus. But think again. Do you know how strange the notion of incarnation was in the ancient Near East? It was an utterly foreign concept. Gods weren't born as helpless children. Gods came about from time immemorial in the ancient world. Gods were begotten of gods as adults with power. There was no tradition in the ancient Near East of a god appearing in any other form except a full-grown adult or in some cases another form of supernatural being.

Nowhere in all of the traditions of the ancient Near East is there a notion that God is born into the world as other than an almighty and powerful God, let alone as a poor child in a manger. Let alone, of a family who is told there is no room for you here. Let alone, someone from the wrong side of the tracks, the Galilee. So, here we have in the doctrine of the incarnation the light of the world in the person of a poor infant. A poor infant from a despised neighborhood. Not a child of standing, not a child of purpose and bearing, but some poor child with a teenage mother. What kind of riffraff is this? Yet there in that stable, of that teenage mother, and with what had to be a shell-shocked Joseph, was born the light of the world.

So, when they ask you in your church, why should we do child advocacy? When they ask you, why should we care about the poor children? This is the Church and after all we have important things to do and to say. Why should we give our time and mission and heartache to child advocacy? You just ask them, are you telling me there's no room for them here? You just ask, how would Jesus have fared under legislation proposing to eliminate benefits for low-income families? Where would Jesus get his inoculations in Toledo, Ohio, today? Where would his people be?

The incarnation is the first and foremost Christian doctrine for a theology of child advocacy: our God came to us as fragile and helpless and vulnerable, poor and despised in a land that was not his own, a stranger in our midst. They say there was no room for God in that stable but it is not so. There was room for God there and there is room in our communities and our churches. Our child advocacy, then, is in the name of a God who breaks into human history. Our child advocacy ministry is in the name and for the sake of the most famous poor child in human history.

The Preferential Option for the Poor

The next Christian doctrine is the preferential option for the poor. Jesus loves poor people. When we talk about this special love, we talk about "the preferential option for the poor." In plain terms, God's special affection for the poor. And we see this over and over again in the Scriptures. Do not send those children away, bring them to me. The woman at the well, on and on and on it goes.

Think about it now with me. Do you remember any story about Jesus healing the powerful regent? I don't recollect that one. Do you remember Jesus saving the rich man so that he could be decked out in the finest jewels and robes? I don't remember that one. I remember Jesus in all the dirty places, all the Samarias. I remember him at a simple wedding changing water to wine, I remember him with a woman who hemorrhaged but had faith and said if I can only touch just the hem of his garment. Just let me draw close enough to touch, and I will be healed. The preferential option for the poor.

To be sure, Hebrew Scripture is replete with references for the poor and the ways we are to live in relation to the poor. This is part of the concern for justice and for mercy that we noted above. Here we want to underscore what appears, by Biblical witness, to be Jesus' deep personal empathy and love of those who are poor, on society's margins. This emphasis on Jesus' part is our focus here. If we live in imitation of Christ, we will exercise a preferential option for the poor.

This whole question of relationship between the powerful and the powerless was revealed to me in an unexpected way. Now, as a mother, what passes for a leisure time activity is doing the Saturday chores. I'm a Calvinist, so I never leave the house without two or three days' worth of reading material, just in case there's a line wherever I'm going. Heaven forbid I should just sit and do nothing.

It was my turn to take the car to the Jiffy Lube. Do you know Jiffy Lube, where you go and they clunk around under the car? I'm not entirely sure what they do but if you don't do it, your car stops or something. I'm not being too technical for you, am I? I don't know, maybe they change liquids. I don't know what they do, but you have to do it sometimes.

Anyway, I took the car and I went in to wait while they did whatever it is they do. To my great horror, I found that I had arrived without any reading material. Now, the Jiffy Lube is something of a male precinct, I've got to say. There was something that I will euphemistically call a coffee table; that is to say, a flat surface, and on it were only two pieces of reading material.

One was a magazine called *Field & Stream*. It's a most peculiar magazine. They sell things in there like worms. Worms. I said worms. By the gross. Now, I'm not really sure how many a gross is, but it's a very lot. I'm having a reasonably happy life. I have never even bought one worm. What do the people do who buy those grosses of worms? It costs you $20 to have a gross of worms and $50 not to have one. They also sell boots that come up to your armpits. I mean, honey, if it's that deep in there, I'd say don't go in. That would be my personal advice.

Well, I pretty soon thought I had about all the enlightenment I could stand from that little publication, so I picked up the other one.

It was the manual that you study when you're getting your boat driver license, like a driver's license for boats. You have to take a test and all that stuff.

Now, I'm a Calvinist, as I already confessed. Calvinists start at the back of the book, and we do that in case we run out of time. We always know how it came out. We don't know what it was about, but we know how it came out.

So, I start at the back, and it's talking about jigs and booms and ta rah rah boomdiyeas, for all I know. I didn't understand much of it.

And then I got to a chapter on the rules for what happens when boats encounter each other on the open sea, in open water, actually, it said. I thought, well, that's kind of interesting. You know, for cars we have traffic lights and traffic lanes and even that doesn't work out all that well. I mean, you may come from a place where you can turn right on a red light, but I work in Manhattan where you can't turn right on a green light. I thought, I wonder how they do that out there on the water where there are no lights or signs or anything. So, I started to read and it said something like this.

There are two kinds of craft. One of them has access to great power. It can accelerate and push its way through the strongest of waves. It can change direction on command. It can even stop on demand. It has great power of its own.

The other class of craft is dependent on the forces of nature, wind, tide, and human effort in paddling, or rowing, or maintenance of the sails.

And these two classes of craft are known as *privileged* and *burdened*. This book said—this is getting pretty interesting, huh? I mean, for a boat story—that these two kinds of craft have two different terms or classes. One class is *privileged* and the other class is *burdened*. But get this, now. The powerful boats, do you think they are considered privileged vessels or burdened? They, my friends, are the burdened vessels. The powerful boats that can make their way forward no matter what, under their own power, they are burdened vessels, burdened with responsibility to give way to the boats without power. And the powerless vessels, the ones that are dependent on the vagaries of tide and wind and weather, they are classified as privileged vessels. To them is accorded the right of way, for if the powerful vessels are not burdened with responsibility for giving way, these powerless vessels may not make safe harbor. Imagine that: the powerful boats are burdened, and the powerless are privileged. And when these two kinds of craft meet each other on the open sea, the privileged and the burdened, the powerful are burdened and must give way if the powerless, the privileged, are ever to make safe harbor.

The powerful must give way if the powerless are ever to make safe harbor.

I thought to myself, who wrote this thing, Billy Graham? Cornel West? Mother Theresa? I turned to the front and it said "New Jersey Department of Transportation." Now, you know what a notable theological institution that is!

Friends, what's going on? What's going on in our land when the Department of Transportation knows that the powerful must give way if the powerless are to make safe harbor—that the powerful are considered burdened and the powerless are privileged—yet the government of the United States and the Church of Jesus Christ are having trouble with the concept.

The Primacy of Children

Another tenet of Christianity is the primacy of children in Jesus' own ministry. Think of the place of children and then read the stories of other gods in the ancient Greek and Hebrew world. You will find stories of salvation and stories of healing but you will not find the primacy of children the way you do in the Gospel of Jesus Christ.

Healing sons and daughters, crippled and mute. Children their parents had given up on. Children no one held out any hope for. The primacy of children in Jesus' own ministry is a remarkable fact of the Gospel. And as child advocates, I hope we will take that to our hearts again and again and again. Who called you into ministry? Jesus' own voice and example called you. You were called into ministry by the living God. By the one who stooped to the smallest child of the ancient Near East. Whom are we to put first? None other than children, for to such as these the kingdom of God belongs. And what does Jesus warn? Better for you to be drowned in the depths of the sea than to put a stumbling block before these little ones. It is the only sanction anywhere in the Gospel accounts of Jesus and it warns us to remove the stumbling blocks that hamper our children.

Sometimes we learn our lessons from unexpected sources. For me, it was a child himself who embodied that doctrine of the primacy of children far better than a lot of adults. For many years, I have worked on the issues of children in pornography and sex tourism, a growing industry around the world. In the course of that work, I was sent to Brazil with a team trying to understand the extent of these problems. We spent days talking to boys aged six, seven, eight, nine who were prostitutes on the streets of Rio, São Paulo, Copacabana Beach, Leblon, and Ipanema.

After several days we went out one evening to see these children. They run like wild dogs; there's no place for them. Nothing for them. Maybe you remember some years ago when the police had had it. The street children were ruining the tourist trade, they said, these riffraff children. And so, they opened their guns and shot them. And then the missionaries came. And they helped. They scooped up all those children and put them in a camp with a twelve-foot chain-link fence with barbed wire on the top. You know what those good folk do? They "let" those children sew soccer balls seventeen hours a day. Our hosts asked, "Shall we go see where the children stay at night?" We went to a highway overpass, where children live under the bridge.

We went to this bridge, and we stayed with these boys, and we brought them food. None of the boys were related to one another, genetically, they were just boys who fell in with one another. The youngest was about three years old; the oldest maybe fourteen. We brought them food and talked long into the night. They were just children, hardened little grown-up children. Children who talked of sex and violence and money and stealing and guns. And then sucked their thumbs as they went to sleep. Children who had no sense of their own age, name, or parentage but who reached out and held hands across a thin blanket of a night.

Late into the night a boy came to join the group. Unlike the other boys, he was not in disheveled clothes. He had a beautiful new haircut and an American-style football shirt with a number and a university name on it. His nails were clean. (I am a mother and I do check these things. His nails were clean.) He had makeup on his face and he was so proud of himself. He had Brazilian money worth three or four U.S. dollars. He had spent eleven or twelve hours being the star of a pornographic film. Selected because he had kind of an American look to him. Given a haircut, scrubbed up, put in clean clothes, and put in a pornographic film.

He had earned a few dollars. I said to him, "What will you do?" He said, "You know I came to rest and eat and be with my friends and tomorrow the first thing we got to do is our baby," that's what they called the three year old, "needs new shoes. He has no shoes. And now I have some money for baby to have shoes. I have some money so baby can have shoes."

I don't know about you. I was thirty years old before I had to worry about buying my baby shoes. And when I did, I pulled my station wagon into the parking space, and I used my credit cards, and I bought baby some shoes without another thought.

Where do we get little children who spend twelve hours in a pornographic film and then go under a bridge? Who are not embittered or hateful or deceitful but who say thank God, I have money to buy baby some shoes? The preferential option for the poor, the weak, the fragile, the vulnerable is a gift from God. The primacy of children is a priority affirmed by none other than Jesus Christ himself. But we have to relieve children like this boy. We have to step up and say we will. Let us not rob his childhood; let us be there. Boys who buy shoes for babies remind us again of what it means to speak of the preferential option for the poor and the primacy of children.

The Doctrine of Love

The seventh doctrine is the doctrine of love. Now, I'm not a great athletic fan but even I know one soccer player by name. Pelé. And why do I remember him? Because on the day at the top of his career when he retired, he came into a packed stadium and he didn't talk about goals or victory or fame, he talked about love. Pelé came into the stadium on the day he retired, and they saluted him as a great soccer player, and they turned to him and asked him if he wanted to speak, and he said to the stadium, "Say it with me, 'Love. Love. Love.'"

Love. That's the quintessential uniqueness of the Gospel. It is about love. It is all about love. We learn in the Gospel that all the other laws are surpassed by this one. Love. Love. Love.

When Marian Wright Edelman and I served the Carter White House during the UN International Year of the Child, I traveled with Mrs. Carter to Chang Mai, Thailand, to a refugee camp. Refugee camps are horrid places. The idea of refugee must be banished. The word *refugee* must become like the word *slave*. It must become a word that describes something that no longer exists because we know better. But it was a refugee camp. These were the days of Pol Pot, the Khmer Rouge, and the killing fields.

As we entered the camp there was a kind of a laundry basket with a little baby in it. The French nuns who provided the nursing care told Mrs. Carter, "This baby's mother walked the baby in but the baby's too small, too little, it was too late. We've given the baby something for pain. The baby can't live, we don't think." We looked at the baby. I never knew whether it was a girl baby or a boy baby. These long years I've always thought of this baby as "string baby" because the baby wore one of those little string caps that are the custom in that part of the world.

We went through that place of human horror and disease and dirt and death and we came out some hours later. And now that little laundry basket had kind of a pillowcase over it. Mrs. Carter, a remarkable First Lady of the United States, came over and knelt down in the mud, laid back the pillowcase, and scooped that baby up into her arms and sat rocking the baby back and forth. The French nurse came to me and asked me to translate for her. She said, "You need to tell your First Lady that baby's gone. The baby couldn't live. The baby died."

I said, "I understand," and I went over and knelt down, and I said, "Mrs. Carter, that baby is gone." She just sat rocking. I said, "The baby's gone, Mrs. Carter. She passed on."

Still rocking the baby, she said, "I know that, Eileen. But this baby's going home to Jesus. It hasn't been loved up enough by our world. I'm going to love this baby on home."

I suggest to you that this is the Gospel's meaning of love. In life or in death, in good times or in bad, the plain fact is our children haven't been loved up enough. Plain fact is we must find a way to take them in our arms to give them grace and succor and to love them on their way. To love them into their journey of faith. And in those terribly sad moments, to love them on home into God's eternal keeping.

The Church as the Body of Christ—An Ecclesiology

The Church as the body of Christ is the next theological idea I want to address. The Church is not supposed to be a commemorative society or a club of like-minded people. It does not say the Church is to be the society that remembers Jesus. But what does Scripture say? To be the *body* of Christ on earth. Think of what our Lord, just before his betrayal and arrest, prayed for. He could have prayed, let me out of this situation, give me a way out, send these men with swords and powers away from me. Get me out of here and back to Galilee. But Scripture says that in his last opportunity to pray, he prayed, "Father let them be one even as You and I are one, even as I am in You and You are in me. So let them be one." And not for his own sake, but why? *So that the world might believe.* For the sake of the world! We must express the oneness that we share in our baptism, "All children of the living God are surely kin to me," as the hymn teaches.

The Church is called to be Christ's body on earth. In imitation of Jesus, the Church will of course worship God, teach God's salvation history, and nurture young and old alike. The Church is called as well to share Jesus' ministries to those who are on the margins of society—the least, the lost, the lonely, the little.

In my thirty years of ecumenical ministry I have had the high privilege of seeing firsthand many of the magnificent congregations whose lives, shaped in imitation of their Christ, bring succor and hope to the communities around them. I think of the large urban church in Newark, New Jersey, that begins every Sunday before dawn when deacons prepare a hearty, hot breakfast and then walk the mean streets to find those who are homeless and hungry and transport them to the church. After breakfast the homeless are offered the comfort of hot showers, hair cuts by volunteer barbers, and clean clothing from a tidy stock of used clothes. Those who wish to remain for worship are given a small amount of money so that they may participate fully in the worship—including the offering.

Or, there is the large West Coast parish in an affluent community that some years ago declared itself a sanctuary church for children. In a busy parish every decision is evaluated with a view to how it will serve the children and their families.

There is the small church in rural Iowa that aids neighboring family farmers through organizing a farm market for the sale of produce, and sponsors after-school care and homework help for community children. This same congregation furnishes the elderly with transportation to distant medical appointments.

Jesus said if you love me, feed my sheep. To be the church is to tend the flock of Jesus—to be present in the lives of those in need.

Koinonia

The New Testament speaks of a kind of deep fellowship between people that is referred to in Greek as *koinonia*. This koinonia points not to what the church or community does but to the quality of the relationships which attend between people. Koinonia points to a kind of community that is forbearing and reflective of deep commitment to one another. The use of the term koinonia in the New Testament is not restricted solely to the church but points to a deep communion of which humans are capable.

When I was growing up it didn't have to be your exact right mother who yelled at you. Do you remember those days? Any old mother would do, you know what I'm saying? Any mother could stop the car and say, "Eileen, put your sweater on, it's getting cold."

"Yes, ma'am," and I would put it on.

What do kids say today? "You're not the boss of me. I don't have to listen to you." And that's to the few adults who still take responsibility for all children; most of us will just look the other way when we see a child in need of any old mother to set them aright.

We have to recover our community. We have to live in a world where any old mom or dad can be responsible for and to any old child. I remember when I was a child, my friend Linda and I were coming home in a snowstorm. We came to a house that had several beagles, and they were out in the yard barking away. Well, we got an idea to throw snowballs at these beagles because they were inside the fence. It seemed like a very good idea at the time. So, we threw snowballs at the beagles. We were littler than our brothers. We both had older brothers. We couldn't throw snowballs at them, they were too good; they not only threw hard, they packed their snowballs hard. Besides that, they could aim. So, we couldn't do that to our big brothers, but these silly beagles, they were jumping up, opening their mouths and it just seemed too good to pass up. So, we threw the snowballs at them.

Then Linda and I came to my home to have hot chocolate. "Oh, no," my mother said, "you'll not be having hot chocolate. You'll be going down the street to apologize to the beagle owners." Well, we did. Seems this poor family had only beagles, no children, so you can imagine how they felt about those beagles.

We apologized. And the people to whom we apologized became friends, neighborhood friends. Do you remember those days when you could do something wrong, face it, admit it, and make a friend? The neighbors were called the Lowells. And the rest of my growing-up days, as I walked past—well, you know, you don't walk past right away, you give it a few weeks to kind of forget how that dog did look with the snowball, but after a time you walk by again. And the rest of my growing-up years, I could walk by, "Morning, Mrs. Lowell, Mr. Lowell."

"Morning, Eileen, how you doing? Things going well?" When I graduated from high school, "We're so proud of you. You have a great future."

We have to return to koinonia, where you don't have to be the exact right mother. Anybody's mother can tell you to put your sweater on and you do so.

The restoration of community. When I worked on the International Year of the Child, it fell to me to go visit a number of states and take these little plastic copies of the Great Seal of the United States to children in Special Olympics.

On one occasion I went to the Special Olympics in Wyoming. If you've never been to a Special Olympics, you owe it to yourself to get to one. In the Special Olympics there were children with braces and crutches and canes, children that were developmentally delayed, children that were physically disabled in one way or another.

It's a wonderful thing to see the foot races. They get to running and if someone falls, which is not an unusual occurrence, the children will say, "Stop, stop." They pick up the one that fell, and then they say, "Okay, ready, set, go." They are athletes. The joy is in the competition, not in the victory.

It was my job to award each participant the Great Seal of the United States on behalf of President Carter. We came to lunch and were sitting at a table. Across from me was a boy who, as the world reckons, had nothing about him that worked right. Legs in braces, little wizened hands, all curled up, wall-eyed, teeth crossed.

He said to me, "Who are you again, are you the president's mother?" These were the days of Miss Lillian Carter, and I shouldn't mind being Miss Lillian, but I said "No, I'm not the president's mother, I'm just the president's friend. He asked me to come see you run and to ask you what he should be doing for the children."

In a heartbeat, this boy that the world reckons doesn't have much of a future said, "Tell the president to feed the poor children. They don't have enough to eat." Koinonia, a sense of community with one another.

You see this boy didn't know that as the world reckons he had no insight. The boy didn't know that he had nothing to share, nothing to contribute. The boy didn't know that wisdom wasn't his. The boy didn't know that he was to be a follower all his life, not a leader.

You know what that boy knew? He knew he had just won a medal from the president. He knew that the president's own mother was there at lunch with him. And he saw a good opportunity to influence policy.

Community, we have to restore community if as a Church and a nation we are to fulfill our calling to care for the children God has entrusted to our care. We have to get back to the place where we all take responsibility for one another.

CHAPTER THREE

The Bible's Witness to Who and Whose We Are

We turn now to the Bible as a resource to child advocacy. Now, I'm a Presbyterian pastor and we Presbyterians, we're really children of the Enlightenment. When a child in the Presbyterian tradition reaches the third grade, we give them a Bible, because we figure that's when they ought to be old enough to read.

My oldest son, Andrew, received his Bible when he entered the third grade. That morning as we were returning home from worship, our two sons were in the back seat of the car. Our younger son was just in kindergarten. He couldn't read much, but he could read his name, Peter. Andrew was thumbing through the Bible and Peter said, "Oh, look, look, it says Peter. It's about me."

Andrew's best friend at the time was a fellow named Mark. Andrew said "Well, I'll read that to you, Peter, but not until I finish this section, it's called the Gossip According to Mark." Well, in a way it is the gossip according to Mark.

I want to suggest some precepts about this book and how we read it, what use it is to us on our journey of child advocacy, and then look at a passage to apply some of those precepts. Then we'll turn to four thematic strains and see how they play out in another passage of scripture, before exploring a range of biblical passages to discern what they tell us about who and whose we are in this ministry of child advocacy.

First, five precepts about the Bible. Number one, **this is a book that is first of all about God**. Like Peter, we like to say this is a story about us and, true enough, it is about us. But before that it is a history of God's determined effort, the salvation history of a God who is determined to have a peaceable kingdom and us in it. This is first of all a book about God. A book that helps us know God, approach God, glimpse God. Only secondarily is it a book about us.

The second precept is that, by and large, **the Bible is not a story addressed to individuals but to communities of people.** This isn't God's word to you; it's God's word to us. Otherwise, we'd all have private Bibles. This is a book addressed to a whole community. In fact, this is a book that *makes* a group of individuals a community. "Once you were no people," says the Lord, "but now you are My people." You are a people, not a random group of individuals rocketing through the universe on your own trajectory, but you are a people and My people.

Third, **this is a book about a journey.** This isn't a book about a destination. It isn't a book that is strictly organized around its characters, but it is a travel journal. It starts, as you know, in the garden of creation. And then there's a flood and in that flood, the people get saved, the animals get saved, but each with their own kind—Lord knows the mosquitoes made it in greater numbers than they ought to have. The Bible does not instruct you to love mosquitoes. But the Bible tells you that God loves mosquitoes.

Anyway, there's that first flood. And they gather two by two, in their own kind, they stick to their own kind. And then comes a sad and weary chapter, slavery in Egypt, followed by a flight into the wilderness in pursuit of the promised land. Then we have the image that there will be a new heaven and a new earth and lions will lie down with lambs. Apparently, we don't go anymore two by two, lions with lions, lambs with lambs. But in this new creation, this long, long trajectory, we come to a place where aardvarks go with lobsters, lions with lambs and, God forgive us, maybe even mosquitoes with Presbyterian pastors.

This is a long saga of a journey, and the secret of the journey is that it matters how you get there. And there's absolutely no evidence you can get there alone. There's absolutely no evidence that you can traverse that journey alone and get where you're going. When you get there, it's going to be the most unbelievable place what with aardvarks and lobsters, lions and lambs.

Fourth, **it's a book that carries its freight in the detail.** There are no minor characters; there are no walk-on roles in this book. There was a multitude of 5,000, that's a big important point. Then there's a little detail: There were some loaves and some fishes. The story is in the detail.

They went to see the baby Jesus and they worshipped him and they praised him and brought him gifts. Then there's a little detail: And an angel of the Lord told them, you go home by another route. Don't you go back that way where Herod's watching; you go on some other way. The story is in the detail. We have to look to the detail.

Fifth, **it's a book best read in faith and in discipline.** We can't just pick up this book willy-nilly. This is not the TV Guide that we just browse and see what might entertain us today. No, we approach this holy sacred text as people of faith.

We've begun to lose that in America. We've got so many books, so many words, so many videotapes. For all I know, somewhere there's a terrible monstrosity of a CliffsNotes of the Bible. We cannot approach this sacred word that way.

Rather, we come to this book in prayer, and that's a discipline we want to accept among ourselves. Let us read this text, such that we pray for illumination. What does that mean? It means before we dare to read these holy words that have guided a people for all of these years that we pray to God that we may hear the message God intends for us to hear. So, we come then in faith and in discipline.

The disbelieving heart finds in this book a series of confusions, crazy things. Banquets where all the invited guests are standing out in the street in their evening clothes and all the riffraff have somehow gotten to the banquet table. The disbelieving heart asks, what kind of story is that? Where is that going to lead you?

The disbelieving heart doesn't read in that sad and sorry history of slavery in Egypt the notion that wherever you are, wherever you are this day, as an individual, as a community, as a nation, you have the dust of Egypt on your feet. You have got to shake it off and get moving down the road, leaving slavery behind you.

The disbelieving heart sees no humor and no humanity. It sees no powerful strain of history in this text but rather a bunch of disjointed stories.

It sees in it stories to be exploited, stories that can be used to justify your bigotries. Doesn't it say women, be silent in the church? Doesn't it say slaves, obey your masters? It is a text that can be exploited and it is a text that can be exalted. And the beloved community exalts this text in faith and in discipline.

The Walk to Emmaus

Let's turn to a text bearing in mind these points: that this is a book about God, it's a book about community, it's a story of a journey. The truth is in the detail and that we approach it in faith and in discipline.

And in that true spirit, as we approach the Scripture, let us pray.

O God, give us fresh ears to hear your word, fresh eyes to see your witness in Scripture, brave hearts to do your will. Attend us now as we attend your word. Stir in us a hunger for your truth and let us hear the words that you would speak to us this day. In the name of the Christ we pray it. Amen.

Let's consider, in light of these precepts, a very interesting story. This is the story found in Luke 24. It is itself a story about a journey. It's called "The Walk to Emmaus."

[13]Now on that same day two of them were going to a village called Emmaus, about seven miles from Jerusalem, [14]and talking with each other about all these things that had happened. [15]While they were talking and discussing, Jesus himself came near and went with them, [16]but their eyes were kept from recognizing him. [17]And he said to them, "What are you discussing with each other while you walk along?" They stood still, looking sad. [18]Then one of them, whose name was Cleopas, answered him, "Are you the only stranger in Jerusalem who does not know the things that have taken place there in these days?"

[19]He asked them, "What things?" They replied, "The things about Jesus of Nazareth, who was a prophet mighty in deed and word before God and all the people, [20]and how our chief priests and leaders handed him over to be condemned to death and crucified him. [21]But we had hoped that he was the one to redeem Israel.

Yes, and besides all this, it is now the third day since these things took place. [22]Moreover, some women of our group astounded us. They were at the tomb early this morning, [23]and when they did not find his body there, they came back and told us that they had indeed seen a vision of angels who said that he was alive. [24]Some of those who were with us went to the tomb and found it just as the women had said; but they did not see him." [25]Then he said to them, "Oh, how foolish you are, and how slow of heart to believe all that the prophets have declared! [26]Was it not necessary that the Messiah should suffer these things and then enter into his glory?" [27]Then beginning with Moses and all the prophets, he interpreted to them the things about himself in all the scriptures.

[28]As they came near the village to which they were going, he walked ahead as if he were going on. [29]But they urged him strongly, saying, "Stay with us, because it is almost evening and the day is now nearly over." So he went in to stay with them. [30]When he was at the table with them, he took bread, blessed and broke it, and gave it to them. [31]Then their eyes were opened, and they recognized him; and he vanished from their sight. (Luke 24:13–31)

Well, what of this story? "On that same day"; well, we know it's Easter day. "Two of them"; we don't know who they are. This is a very important story and we have no idea who these people are. Two of them. Now a little later in the text we learn that one of them is called Cleopas. We don't know who the other one is. Now, I don't believe it's exegetically, interpretively incorrect to suggest that what have here is a story about Mr. and Mrs. Cleopas. I mean, they're walking home and they're going to get something to eat. All I know is he had better not be bringing home someone to dinner unannounced. This had better be Mrs. Cleopas! And in these days we can't call ahead.

So, I think maybe this is Mr. and Mrs. Cleopas. They're walking to Emmaus. Well, we have that detail, Emmaus. Emmaus is about seven miles from Jerusalem. It seems that Mr. and Mrs. Cleopas come from a bad neighborhood. It is seven miles from Jerusalem, nowhere near the center of power. They live over across the tracks, in some old Emmaus—someplace where you've got to walk. And when it's your suppertime you got to get back in your neighborhood. You don't be walking into just any old restaurant anywhere.

So, these two folks are walking along and they're talking about the things that had happened. This is that first Easter day. They don't know how to understand recent events. They don't understand what has befallen their community. They believed in their teacher, and he was crucified, and there's this confusing story, and they're just jabbering away, Mr. and Mrs. Cleopas, trying to figure it all out.

"While they were talking and discussing, Jesus came near and went with them." Not walked up to them and stopped them. They're walking home to dinner. This man comes up and he *walks with* them.

Then this verse, a very important verse: "but their eyes were kept from recognizing him." Now, it doesn't say they were blinded. So, we don't think this is an ophthalmological problem. He's not in a disguise. For sure it would tell us that, you know, if he had one of those Groucho masks. He's not in somebody else's robes or something, but "their eyes were kept from recognizing him." Must be in the detail here—something is keeping them from recognizing him. Maybe this plot is going to thicken. Maybe we're going to find out why they were kept from recognizing.

"And Jesus said, 'What are you discussing with each other while you walk along?' They stood still, looking sad." It seems, doesn't it, that it's hard to recognize Jesus if you're standing still looking sad. Must be that if you want to recognize Jesus, you can't stand still looking sad. Must be that you have to look some other way and you have to be on the move.

They stood still looking sad. Then one of them, Mr. Cleopas (fools rush in where angels fear to tread), Mr. Cleopas answers him, maybe with some irritation, "Are you the only stranger in Jerusalem who does not know [what's going on]?"

Think of one of those awful days that everyone remembers: September 11th or the day President Kennedy was shot. Can you imagine someone walking in and saying, what's going on? Wouldn't you say, are you the only person in America who doesn't know?

Remember the day of Columbine; we walked around heartsick all day. And if someone had said, good afternoon, how are you doing, what's going on today? Wouldn't we say, are you the only person— what planet are you from?

Remember the day Dr. King was shot and you felt as if time itself stood still, like even the trees and the grass were going to respond? Imagine in those moments someone walks up to you and says, what are you talking about? in this breezy kind of way.

And what are you going to respond? Are you the only person, are you kidding, do you not know what has taken place here? Are you that far behind the door, do you not read a paper, do you not have television and radio? And anyway what are you doing on this poor road to this poor neighborhood asking such questions?

We're poor people going home in confusion and hunger. There must be some reason we can't eat in Jerusalem, so we're making our way to Emmaus. Anybody could eat in Emmaus, we're poor folk.

And this man walks up, we don't recognize him, and he's asking this question. So Cleopas tells him about Jesus of Nazareth and what happened. He was arrested and the leaders took him away. And in verse 21 he says—again this detail—"But we had hoped that he was the one to redeem Israel."

Don't you know they say to the man that they can't recognize, we had all our hopes pinned on him. It was in him that we hoped there was salvation for our society. It was in him that we believed we would come to that peaceable kingdom. It was in him that we dared to believe there would be peace and justice. He was the hope of Israel.

They say to this stranger, Sir, can't you tell our hopes have died? Hope itself has shriveled up inside us and gone away. Yes, yes, says Cleopas, and worse than that, not only is our hope dead, not only are we afraid of the chief priests, not only are we afraid of the Roman authorities, but worse than that, "some women of our group astounded us." Doesn't that just figure?

Some women in our group astounded us. I believe that's sort of a lingering issue in the human community. We still have women in our group who astound us.

He goes on to explain how the women astound—these women were at the tomb early this morning and they did not find his body there. And they came back and told us that they had indeed seen a vision of angels who said that he was alive. Now, this is truly complicated. These women have gone to the tomb to care for the body in the way that women in our culture do. They were going to pour ointments, and they had new shrouds, and they were going to see to the burial of this body. And they went there. Now, maybe they got the wrong tomb. I mean, there's no telling just what has happened. Maybe they got to talking and went right straight past the tomb. It was a new rock in the front and they didn't recognize it. I mean, who does know?

So, these women went, but they couldn't find the body. Did they come back and say, look, can you give us those directions again, we seem to have made a wrong turn? Did they come back and say, we went, but we couldn't find the right tomb? No, they didn't own up to it. They came back with a preposterous story. They came back and said, "His body's gone." Well, if they had come back and just said that, we'd have said grave robbers came and took him away.

But they didn't even come and just say that, these women. They came with such a story, they said we got to the right tomb, we followed all the directions, we turned at the third sarcophagus, we got that tomb with the new rock, we went in and the body was gone. We were distressed, but then angels, messengers from God came and they said, He's not here. He's alive. Not only is he not here but he is alive. There is no body to be found. You're looking in the wrong place, you're snooping among the dead and he's alive. You're looking among the corpses and he's on the road again. He's on the way to Emmaus. He's going to go to Galilee, go catch up with him. So, the women come back.

Well, Cleopas is recounting this to this stranger on the road. He says, "Some of those who were with us"—now, he just told Jesus that the women came with this preposterous story. So, "some of those who were with us," means some of those MEN, some of those BROTHERS who were with us. Now look, we got this crazy story, we better send somebody reliable to see what's happening here. That's what it means. We'll send somebody better, send somebody reliable, credible, who won't get lost amid the sarcophagi, who won't come back with some crazy story. You send some men. They know how to find that dead body.

But listen here, "Some of those who were with us went to the tomb," some of the men, "And found it just as the women had said; but they did not see him." So, the men left. This is Cleopas and he's telling this, this is the worst day of our lives don't you know, stranger. We got crazy stories, we got fear, hope has died.

And then Jesus says, this risen Christ says, "Oh, how foolish you are, and how slow of heart to believe."

Now, that's a very interesting use of the word *heart*. What if this text said, "Oh, how foolish you are and how slow of mind," but it says nothing about mind, does it? It says "how slow of heart."

This risen Christ doesn't believe you learn things through your mind. He probably doesn't know that there are people that we have deemed uneducable. He is talking about heart, not mind.

"How slow of heart to believe all that the prophets have declared!" And did the prophets not tell you there would come a day, a day like this, when humanity can start again? Did the prophets not tell you there would come a time when justice would roll down like a mighty stream?

Jesus goes on, "Was it not necessary that the Messiah should suffer these things and then enter into his glory?" This stranger on the road that they don't recognize says, didn't you know, didn't you remember that the Messiah would come and suffer and conquer death, so we would again look at death and laugh the great belly laugh of those who know that it's defeated?

Now, the very interesting verse here, "Then beginning with Moses," that's going a long way back, especially for some folks stopped on a hot road. It's only seven miles after all, even if Mr. Cleopas is giving the directions.

"Then beginning with Moses and all the prophets, [Jesus] interpreted to them the things about himself in all the scriptures." All the things. He told them what was what.

Now, as a twentieth-century pastor, I'd like to ask, why didn't somebody write that down? We have no text. No manuscript. You'd think with Jesus saying all that—something that important—somebody could have made a note or two. Mrs. Cleopas could have put it on the back of her grocery list. Mr. Cleopas could have put it on his laundry tag, made a couple notes.

But, no, the detail, the detail, the detail. Why is that? Such an important story that Jesus told them from Moses through the prophets to his own time. Why didn't anybody write it down?

Maybe this risen Christ believed every generation must learn it for themselves. Maybe—maybe he said don't write this down. I have to tell you something, but don't write this down. Off the record, keep it quiet, just between us. Just between us.

Because there will come another walk on another road to another Emmaus and they must learn it for themselves. There will come another time when poor people are headed back to their neighborhood accompanied by the risen Lord and they will recognize among themselves the truth. Don't write this down. Let's just go on background on this one.

Well, this stunning walk to Emmaus—"As they came near the village to which they were going, [Jesus] walked ahead as if he were going on." Now, that's the polite thing to do, isn't it? They were coming home to their own little home. So, as a guest you want to hurry along, so they don't feel obliged to offer what meager food they have. It's only polite to say, not me, I'm not hungry. Not me, I've got places to go. It's only polite to let them have their peace and privacy.

And, so, Jesus is a polite host and a polite guest. He moves along as if to go, but the Cleopas family "urge[s] him strongly." Now, they still don't recognize him. He's this man with wild questions and even wilder answers. They say, "Stay with us, because it is almost evening and the day is now nearly over." Don't you see, it's going to get dark, don't you know where you are? This is Emmaus. You don't walk around here after dark, especially some person with all these crazy questions. You go around with your crazy questions in this dark neighborhood, you're going to come to some bad end. Don't you be going. Mrs. Cleopas said, Cleopas, get this poor fool and bring him in the house. He's going to get himself killed. She doesn't know he already did that.

She said, this fool is going to walk around. He doesn't know this is Emmaus, bring him in the house, for heaven's sakes, dear, we'll find something to fix for dinner.

"So he went in to stay with them." He came to their table at their urging. Again the detail. Have you been urging Christ in to your table? Have you said, come in here and stay with us? Have you been urging him to stay, to linger a while?

He came at their urging. "So he went in to stay with them." And they washed up, they found a little something, put it on the table and "when he was at the table with them, he took bread, blessed and broke it, and gave it to them." He gave it to them. He gave it to them. Whose house is this? Whose bread is this? He gave it to *them*. He *gave* it to them. They didn't give it to him. He gave it to them.

Then in the breaking of bread, in that fellowship around that rude table, with that simple banquet of bread, "their eyes were opened, and they recognized him." My Lord and my God, look who's sitting at the table. Oh, Cleopas, look who we brought home. What have we done now?

My God, he is alive. Lord, the women were right. "He took bread, blessed, and broke it, and gave it to them. Then their eyes were opened, and they recognized him." And the last of that verse: "and he vanished from their sight." You only get a glimpse. But you know it when you see it.

Now, show me the child advocate who can't be helped by the simple truths of this story. Let's review just those few little points. You might find yourself as child advocates on a road to a bad neighborhood. It could be a bad neighborhood like we call a bad neighborhood in a city, kind of a lower East Side or a South Central or—you know what you call it in your community.

Or it could be a truly bad neighborhood, we're talking U.S. Senate here. I mean, you could be mixing with some really dangerous people.

You could be mixing in some places where your mother would not wish you to be. You could be in the place where people are thinking of taking their own lives or somebody else's. You'll be in that very, very tough neighborhood, really rough neighborhood.

You could be on the way to a lot of bad places even if it be only seven miles or so from the good places you ought to be. People will come up to you when you're trying to do your best in your child advocacy with questions that are frankly off the wall, asking you all sorts of questions. Sometimes you're very wound up in your policy matter and some silly woman's coming here asking you about her child. Doesn't she know you're working on the mark-up session? Doesn't she know you're thinking about Senator Hm-hm and what he's going to do and she's in your face about Jason or Sally, Tyrone or Laticia? She wants to know, what's going to happen to my child? Sometimes we will be asked peculiar questions in the face of a stranger and the challenge to the child advocate is to ask, could this stranger be the one we believed he might be?

Then if you get in that bad neighborhood with the senators and so on, they're going to tell you, This is a good bill, the best we can do. Better than we ought, better than I thought. Aren't you grateful to me? Don't you buy that, don't you buy that.

Well, so we go along in this story and the child advocate might recognize that it's very hard to recognize Jesus when you're standing still looking sad. Don't we get defeated sometimes? Don't you come just grinding to a halt in the middle of the road some days, just bone weary of telling the same people the same things, things they ought to know and have taken to heart long since? Don't you ever get just bone weary and start standing still and looking sad?

Well, a primary lesson of this text is that no matter what else is true, this is true and sure: you cannot recognize the Christ when you're standing still looking sad. You sing your way out of that mess, or you pray your way out of that mess, or you work your way out of that mess, but don't you stand still because it's sure you will not recognize the Christ standing still, looking sad.

This place, and in every place we find ourselves, is the home of our movement, it is our neighborhood. And in our neighborhood we must look around to see if any of our folk have skittered to a halt. See if we notice one in our midst who's kind of ground to a stop, put our arm around them, remind them, whisper in their ear, "You can't recognize him standing still, looking sad. Come with me. We'll go on ahead to the place where there's a table. A table where we break bread, a simple meal, a cup, a loaf, an opportunity to be with one another and to be in the whole communion of saints and there we will recognize the Christ."

Well, there you have it. Reading the Bible with a keen eye to detail, a notion of the journey, a sense that it is more about God than it is about us, this isn't a story about the Cleopas family, this is a story about the way in which God comes to us, and not just us as individuals but us as a community. And it's approached always in faith and in discipline.

Four Thematic Strains

We looked at the nature of how we read this Bible, how we take to ourselves this good Word. And we identified five precepts: that this is a book that is essentially about God. It's addressed not to individuals primarily but to communities. It is a saga of traveling people, a journey story. One must look to the detail, and that it's best read in faith and in discipline.

I want to accompany our five precepts with four thematic strains we will expect to find in the word of God.

The first thematic strain is the **persistence of God's love**. In your mother's womb I knew you, from the first you were mine. In my own image have you been created.

Our wonderful, contemporary prophet Desmond Tutu addressing the somewhat struggling Afrikaaner Church came to that place, to the Afrikaaner Church, the Church that had dared to speak God's blessing on the evil of apartheid. And did Desmond Tutu bring a word of justice, a stern word of warning? Desmond Tutu, diminutive, little Desmond Tutu, came among them with this word. "Brothers and sisters in Christ," he said, "there is nothing you can do to make God love you more."

To the purveyors of apartheid Desmond Tutu said, "There is nothing—nothing you can do to make God love you more." Imagine that. Many of us, armchair quarterbacks, sat back and said, that's a tactical error. He ought to be pointing out that they must repent and recant from apartheid.

And it probably is a tactical error. Desmond Tutu, it seems, doesn't play by the tactical rules. He plays by the rules in another playbook, the persistence of the love of God.

So, he said to them, come let us rule together, live together, worship together and thrive together in a free South Africa. But know this, there's nothing you can do to make God love you more. God already loves you. You are beloved, you cannot do anything to make God love you more. The persistence of God's love.

Second, the **relentlessness of God's justice and mercy.** Throughout this book we will see over and over again that justice does not come along without its twin, mercy. They simply do not leave each other's company in this book. Where we find justice, we find mercy. Where we find mercy, we find justice. They do not leave each other. They are, as they say in the medical realm, conjoined twins. They have no viable life divided from one another. Here we find judging the peoples with equity coexisting with the promise to remember our sins no more.

Third, we will find the **omnipotence of God's capacity** throughout this book. The human nature leads itself into an inescapable corner where there is absolutely no way out. But the Biblical witness to the omniscience, the all-powerful nature of God and God's capacity, repeatedly, time after time, finds a way out of no way.

And, fourth, the one we have trouble with, we will find a thematic strain that calls our attention to the **necessity and efficacy of human agency.** That is to say, we are called, in the Hebrew Scriptures and in the New Testament, to be workmates to God in the redemption of the cosmos. We are not bystanders, we are not they who hold orchestra seats, who are there to watch. We are not there to sing the hymns, to provide a little musical accompaniment to God's redemption. We are to take the gift and the goal of redemption into our own hearts and lives and to witness to it. We do not create redemption, that's God's agency; human agency is witnessing to it.

Potsherds and Witnesses

So, let's turn to Scripture with which to illustrate these themes, beginning with Second Corinthians.

> [7]But we have this treasure in clay jars, so that it may be made clear that this extraordinary power belongs to God and does not come from us. [8]We are afflicted in every way, but not crushed; perplexed, but not driven to despair; [9]persecuted, but not forsaken; struck down, but not destroyed;

^{10}always carrying in the body the death of Jesus, so that the life of Jesus may also be made visible in our bodies. ^{11}For while we live, we are always being given up to death for Jesus' sake, so that the life of Jesus may be made visible in our mortal flesh. ^{12}So death is at work in us, but life in you.

^{13}But just as we have the same spirit of faith that is in accordance with scripture—"I believed, and so I spoke"—we also believe, and so we speak, ^{14}because we know that the one who raised the Lord Jesus will raise us also with Jesus and will bring us with you into his presence. ^{15}Yes, everything is for your sake, so that grace, as it extends to more and more people, may increase thanksgiving, to the glory of God.

^{16}So we do not lose heart. Even though our outer nature is wasting away, our inner nature is being renewed day by day. ^{17}For this slight momentary affliction is preparing us for an eternal weight of glory beyond all measure. (2 Cor. 4:7–17).

When my husband and I graduated from seminary—and there are few things more dangerous than newly minted pastors—we went on an ecumenical journey to the Middle East as short-term mission workers.

We were eager. Eager to teach, too eager. Eager to learn, but not eager enough. We arrived in that holy land and we lived in Cairo, Beirut, and Jerusalem. We went to the museums, one after the other. And as we walked into the museums, I don't know what we had in mind. We probably had in mind these interactive museums that we have here in North America. Not so in the Middle East. There we found just one dusty room after another.

In each room, for example, in Damascus, just off the street called Straight is the museum, and you walk in there ready to be inspired, ready to look at the artifacts. And you come upon a case with broken potsherds. It says 8th Century B.C. (before the Common Era).

So, we looked at potsherds, we gave it attention, though there's only so much attention one can give a potsherd. And then we walked on to the next room where the glad news met us that here were housed potsherds from the first century A.D. or, as many say now, C.E. (Common Era). Well, they might have been used by our Lord, so we gave them our attention.

And then we moved into the third room, ready for other things, only, our luck, it is in this room that the potsherds of the fourth century are kept.

What are potsherds? Well, they're little pieces—those of you who have children or grandchildren under five don't need to hear this—potsherds are what happen when somebody's reaching too enthusiastically for the biscuits. Potsherds are broken pieces of pottery, just daily pots and pans and dishes and bowls. Potsherds.

And Paul dares to say, we are clay jars, earthen vessels. We will shatter in a minute, we will go to pieces in an instant, left to our own devices, and they will have us scattered through a hundred rooms in preservation.

Paul says this, but there's something else. Because of Christ's redeeming acts, we are afflicted in every way, but we are not crushed. This day there will be no potsherds from us. This day they'll put the pressure on the pot, but it will not give. It will be dropped to the floor, but it will not shatter, because we are afflicted in every way, but we are not crushed. Paul gives us a whole litany. We're afflicted but we're not crushed, we're perplexed but we're not despairing. Persecuted, those random acts of human outrage, those bigotries about race or clan or age or style, we are persecuted, but we're not forsaken, we're not alone. We can even be struck down, says Paul, and we will not be destroyed. Because God is with us, redeeming us moment to moment, accompanying us moment to moment, saying poor earthen vessels, hang on, hang on to all your parts. Be whole. Do not be crushed, afflicted though you may be. The persistence of God's love.

Well, I thought I was being a little hard on potsherds. And then I read Paul. We are struck down, but not crushed.

I have seen what that means firsthand in a young man who moved to a new community when he was in sixth grade. At school people would talk to Anthony, ask him what class he was going to now. And Anthony would draw his breath, look at the person who asked the question, and in the most painful stammer anyone had ever heard, say "I'm ggggoing to science class nnnnow."

It was so painful to talk to him that people actually stopped talking to Anthony. They quickly rounded up the speech therapist, and she took him away for a day or so to try to diagnose what the problem was. This boy had just come into the school district.

She came back to the faculty two days later. She said, "I've had a good chance to review Anthony's speech problems. He doesn't have a classic stammer. Anthony's parents are both deaf and mute, so Anthony's first language is American Sign Language. When we force him to speak in our idiom, he can't make it work." In essence, he wasn't needing an English as a second language class, but a kind of *speaking* as a second language class.

Well, some wise and kind teacher suggested that each teacher who Anthony had that year should explain his bilingualness to his classmates and invite him, whenever he spoke, to both sign and speak at the same time. In time Anthony became a proficient speaker.

At his high school graduation, Anthony took the podium. By then he could speak easily with or without signing. It was, as high school speeches go, neither better nor worse than most. He thanked the faculty, made a few jokes, said a few words of encouragement to his classmates.

But the real joy, his parents were sitting in the front with a signer there. People who are deaf, of course, don't clap for others when they are pleased by a speaker, because they can't hear that. When they appreciate something, to applaud they raise their hands and wiggle their fingers. When Anthony concluded his remarks, his parents applauded in their fashion and all the other parents clapped. But the real lesson of that day was when his classmates rose as one and with raised hands and wiggling fingers saluted Anthony's efforts in a language his parents could "hear."

We can be crushed, we can be struck down, but we do not despair, we do not give up, and we do not cease to believe that God is with us. The persistence of God's love.

In this consideration of potsherds and witnesses, let's turn now to another passage by which to illustrate these themes.

> Therefore, since we are surrounded by so great a cloud of witnesses, let us lay aside every weight and the sin that clings so closely, and let us run with perseverance the race that is set before us, [2]looking to Jesus the pioneer and perfecter of our faith, who for the sake of the joy that was set before him endured the cross, disregarding its shame, and has taken his seat at the right hand of the throne of God. [12]Therefore lift your drooping hands and strengthen your weak knees, [13]and make straight paths for your feet, so that what is lame may not put out of joint, but rather be healed. (Hebrews 12:1–2, 12–13)

In this work of faithful child advocacy, we are indeed surrounded by a cloud of witnesses. At CDF's Haley Farm we have each other but also we have the spiritual presence of others. I thought I saw Miss Fannie Lou, with her fierce dignity, walk by. I thought Rev. Prathia Hall, recently gone home, tarried by here. I believe Dr. King might have stopped by to hear Fred Shuttlesworth one more time. And did we not sense them—they had us surrounded, didn't they—because when we gather, all the rest come. The communion of saints attends us as we run this race.

When we gather, all the rest always come. They come and stand by us. They stand around us. And on our wobbliest days, they stand right in us, so that we can stand, surrounded as we are by so great a cloud of witnesses.

Remember we said it's in the details. "Let us run with perseverance." Now, brothers and sisters, do you hear any word about speed in there? Races are intended to be run fast. That's how you win.

Now, I'm not a woman built for speed. I'm so very grateful that it doesn't say anything about speed or velocity in this passage. Doesn't say anything about speed, does it? It doesn't say get there first, beat out your competition; it says persevere.

And it says run in a crowd, "since we are surrounded by so great a cloud of witnesses." Now, if there's one thing that's not pretty, it's a group trying to run all together. That's no way to run. You get out front or you make your strategy or you lay back and then you pour it on in the closing yards.

This says run in a crowd. Get them all around you. You all go at once. Be a movement. You're not Roger Bannister, you're not going for the world record. You all go at once, surrounded by so great a cloud of witnesses.

"Therefore lift your drooping hands." Do you love this, that this writer knows about us? He's seen our drooping hands. Seen our weak knees and knows that we need to be told we have permission now to lift those drooping hands and those weak knees.

So, these themes briefly: the persistence of God's love; the relentlessness of God's justice and mercy; the omnipotence, the endlessness of God's capacity; and the absolutely necessity of human agency. Let us then be afflicted in every way, but, no, we will not be crushed. And surround ourselves with a cloud of witnesses and run with perseverance, all that great cloud of witnesses.

Now, I want to go back to that business of potsherds, those poor clay vessels. I want to remind us of two things. In 1959 a goatherd—

not a herd of goats but a goatherd, like a shepherd for goats—saw some pieces of potsherd on the ground and he followed them.

They led him into a cave and inside the cave were the Dead Sea Scrolls, the return to the community of faith of so many things that we had lost. Potsherds, clay pots, earthen vessels, us.

One last note about potsherds. In those rooms, you know, room after room after room of potsherds from the eighth century, from the first century, from the fourth century, yes, it was tedious. Yes, there were many of them. Yes, they all looked more or less the same to this untutored eye. But I point out to you it took room after room to mark their place. It took no room at all in those museums to house the remains of great temples and palaces, for there were none. Just potsherds.

Asking, So What?

Even when we bear in mind the precepts we have discussed concerning how we see the Bible and how we approach it, we still have a way to go before its meaning becomes clear to us. All that we do in Bible study is intended to address that most profound and simple of all questions, So what?

So, now we ask the all-important question and it's a very complicated, theologically astute question. The question we ask of the text now is: So, what does it mean? What does it instruct? What does it teach? What does it say? So what?

The One Who Knows Who We Are

The texts we will explore are Psalm 139 and Mark 2. And as befits the people of God, as we approach this holy word, let us join our hearts and minds in prayer.

Oh, God, source of all light, by Your word You give light to the soul. Amid all the changing words of our generation, speak Your eternal word that does not change, that we may respond to Your gracious promise with faithful and obedient lives through Jesus Christ, our Lord Amen.

The 139th Psalm, a psalm of David, a psalm of that shepherd who would be king. Let us attend then to the word.

O Lord, you have searched me and known me.

²You know when I sit down and when I rise up; you discern my thoughts from far away.

³You search out my path and my lying down, and are acquainted with all my ways.

⁴Even before a word is on my tongue, O Lord, you know it completely.

⁵You hem me in, behind and before, and lay your hand upon me.

⁶Such knowledge is too wonderful for me; it is so high that I cannot attain it.

⁷Where can I go from your spirit? Where can I flee from your presence?

⁸If I ascend to heaven, you are there; if I make my bed in Sheol, you are there.

⁹If I take the wings of the morning and settle at the farthest limits of the sea,

¹⁰even there your hand shall lead me, and your right hand shall hold me fast.

¹¹If I say, "Surely the darkness shall cover me, and the light around me become night,"

¹²even the darkness is not dark to you; the night is as bright as the day, for darkness is as light to you.

¹³For it was you who formed my inward parts; you knit me together in my mother's womb.

¹⁴I praise you, for I am fearfully and wonderfully made. Wonderful are your works; that I know very well.

¹⁵My frame was not hidden from you, when I was being made in secret, intricately woven in the depths of the earth.

¹⁶Your eyes beheld my unformed substance. In your book were written all the days that were formed for me, when none of them as yet existed.

¹⁷How weighty to me are your thoughts, O God! How vast is the sum of them!

¹⁸I try to count them—they are more than the sand; I come to the end—I am still with you. (Psalm 139:1–18)

The psalm goes on to a prayer of lament, and we'll return to that in a moment. But think of those precepts, the constancy of God, the omnipotence of God's capacity, and the notion of God's absolute immutable love. We hear in those words a double mirror: we are hearing the psalm of David, who celebrates the way in which his creator God knows him, and in so doing, the shepherd tells us how well he knows his God.

It's a double mirror. Have you been in one of those mirror fun houses? Now, that's using a broad definition of fun! I have followed my children into those mirrored things and, of course, my sons whip right through as children will. I smash into every glass wall all the way along, making a scene of myself. Finally one of them comes back and fetches me through.

This is that kind of passage. We think we see it over there, but it's over here. We think we hear David describing the God he knows, and so he is. But in so doing, David describes his own heart. He's describing himself as well.

The great hymnist Charles Tinley was so inspired by this Psalm that it was the inspiration for his well-known hymn, "Stand By Me." Charles Tinley read this psalm and meditated upon it at the time of the loss of his own child.

Hear these two verses, "In the midst of tribulation, stand by me. In the midst of tribulation, stand by me. When I do the best I can and my friends misunderstand, thou who never lost a battle, stand by me."

Where can I go to outrun the Lord? If I ascend to heaven, you are there. If I slip under the cloak of evening fall, there is no darkness and no shadow to you.

Again in Tinley's words, "In the midst of persecution, stand by me. In the midst of persecution, stand by me. When my foes in battle array undertake to stop my way, thou who saved Paul and Silas, stand by me."

This double mirror, this 139th Psalm, helped David to articulate his beliefs, his theology of God, his understanding of God. It helps us still, helps us give word to our thoughts of God.

It has inspired those ever since, like Charles Tinley. This sense of knowledge and identity. That's the theme we talked about earlier.

The constancy of God's love running through the Bible like a steel rod is the concept. Don't worry. You belong to me. Once you were no people, but now you are My people. You will never be forsaken and alone.

Recalling our EMT analogy for taking a spiritual assessment, I suggest to you this shepherd says to us today, brothers and sisters, be alert and conscious times four. Know who and whose you are. Know where you are. Know what time it is. And know what just happened.

Come into your alert conscious state, you know who you are and what that means. That means know whose you are. To whom you belong. That's our identity.

The one to whom we belong tells us don't worry. You know, we do—we waste so much energy in our worry, don't we? When we worry, it doesn't actually rob tomorrow of its sorrow. It robs today of its joy. Worrying doesn't relieve the sorrow of tomorrow, but it surely empties today of its joy. As we move to craft a theology, to discern and construct a theology for this moment in child advocacy, we must be alert and conscious times four.

We know who we are. We're not somebody else. We are the people of God. We are not gladiators in the cultural wars. We have been down that road and wasted way too much energy. Ours is a higher calling. In 1947, a year before his death, Mahatma Gandhi said, "Non-cooperation with evil is as much a duty as is cooperation with good."

It will not be easy. All around us the culture suggests to us alternative identities. Have a look at the television, especially the commercials. Most of the commercials are dedicated to making you something that you aren't. Most of them suggest that you ought to have a different color hair, different physique, different clothing, and a different smell. (Maybe not such a bad idea.) None of them say remember who you are today when you go out. None of them say buy my product so that you can reassert who you are.

They are pandering an alternative faith structure. They are pandering to us and to our children an alternative faith structure that says you can be a god. You have no need of God, you can become a god. You can reshape yourself, reform yourself, wear the right sneakers, eat the right flakes in the morning, and you shall *become* a god. In fact, the subtext of that advertisement is, forget who you are. Forget who you are. Reinvent yourself.

The Church of Jesus Christ is called to stand in resistance and say, be alert and conscious. Know who you are, know where you are, know that you are at ground zero of the cultural wars. Know that you are in a place where they will turn your head left or right and try to dissuade you from your true identity.

They will try to make you worried and anxious. All throughout Scripture there are these little, some would say, platitudes tucked in. Consider the lilies, do not worry. Consider the birds of the air.

There is a Scandinavian proverb that says worry gives a small thing a big shadow. Scripture says let not a shadow be cast. Let not a shadow be cast.

The 139th Psalm closes with a lament. David prays, God, smite my enemies. God, do away with the wicked and most especially, God, remember that when people hated you, I hated them back. This is King David, the early years. This is the boy who would be king, but in this section of the Psalm he sees not God reflected but some lesser king—he sees himself in all his florid revengeful wrath.

David was mistaken. The only person you ought to get even with is the one that did you a good turn. The only one worth squaring up accounts with is the one who was there for you when you were in need.

The person who pursues revenge ought to dig two graves. If you're going after revenge, then dig yourself two graves, because you're going to bury yourself, too.

Being the Body of Christ: The Necessity of Human Agency

I want to move on to Mark's account. It's an early account of a crippled man and his friends. Now sometimes preachers make it sound as if salvation is an incantation. Just say the name "Jesus" and it is all accomplished.

They seldom speak of the role of humanity in accomplishing the design of our great God. It's a kind of drive-through view of salvation. Drive through, pick up your God, and go out the exit. Salvation assured.

The God whom we worship and adore says you will be the body of Christ on earth and invites us into the co-creation of the new heaven and the new earth. Not only invites us in—God commands us into this work. In the words of Dr. Otis Moss Jr., "There is no wrong time to do a right thing." It can't be off schedule. God calls us to live and by our own agency show the love of God that is in Jesus in service to the restoration of the peaceable kingdom.

Well, here's the nature of this restoration of wholeness. This is a story that's contained in all three Synoptic gospels. Mark places it in the second chapter, very early in Jesus' public ministry.

When he returned to Capernaum after some days, it was reported that he was at home. ²So many gathered around that there was no longer room for them, not even in front of the door; and he was speaking the word to them. ³Then some people came, bringing to him a paralyzed man, carried by four of them. ⁴And when they could not bring him to Jesus because of the crowd, **they removed the roof above him**; and after having dug through it, they let down the mat on which the paralytic lay. ⁵When Jesus saw their faith, he said to the paralytic, "Son, your sins are forgiven." ⁶Now some of the scribes were sitting there, questioning in their hearts, ⁷"Why does this fellow speak in this way? It is blasphemy! Who can forgive sins but God alone?" ⁸At once Jesus perceived in his spirit that they were discussing these questions among themselves; and he said to them, "Why do you raise such questions in your hearts?" (Mark 2:1–8, emphasis added)

Jesus doesn't say, why didn't you confront me with that? He asks, how did that even come to blossom inside your breast? Could you not just rejoice that the man was healed? How in the world did a question arise in your heart?

Then Jesus says to the scribes,

⁹"Which is easier, to say to the paralytic, 'Your sins are forgiven', or to say, 'Stand up and take your mat and walk'? ¹⁰But so that you may know that the Son of Man has authority on earth to forgive sins"—he said to the paralytic—¹¹"I say to you, stand up, take your mat and go to your home." ¹²And he stood up, and immediately took the mat and went out before all of them; so that they were all amazed and glorified God, saying, "We have never seen anything like this!" (Mark 2:9–12)

Indeed, they never had.

I want to suggest that imbedded in this story, most particularly in the detail of the story, is direction for beginning to construct a theology that will sustain us.

Today, it's fashionable to deconstruct theology. It's very fashionable to debunk the myths. Well, don't debunk them too readily. We need those myths. Myth in that sense is an account that is at once fanciful and capturing of the truth. It expresses a truth that is inexpressible in a linear fashion.

We do not need to debunk or deconstruct this account. We need to hear it. Let's just look at that scene again. Word went around town the man was home. It was reported that he was at home. At Buckingham Palace, whenever the queen is there, they raise the flag. Word goes around. She's at home. In this setting of Capernaum, word had gotten around town that Jesus was in residence. He's receiving, got folks coming. And so many had gotten that word and they all crowded to the front door. Jesus was talking with them and no more people could fit into the house.

Then some people came—and this is where I want us to give our kindest and most thorough attention—some people came to him bringing to him a paralyzed man. You see, it seems in the detail of the story that some folks can't get to Jesus under their own steam. It seems that some can't get there unless the rest of us carry them.

Maybe there are some days you can't get there yourself without a little help. Well, now here's the shocking part. I'm not so good with numbers, but even I know that there was one paralyzed man and it took four to bring him to Jesus. By a factor of at least four, we must find those to carry children to Jesus. I don't know how many children you love, but however many you have, however many you pray for and care about, multiply that by four. That is how many caring, committed, concerned adults or advocates they need. Because sometimes you just plain have to be carried to Jesus. You can't get there under your own steam.

Now, let's talk about the character and nature of these four. Are these four nice souls who were willing to help a paralytic, poor soul, who couldn't get to Jesus, apt to humbly stand for hours out in the yard waiting their turn to see Jesus? Oh, no. Oh, no. They took one look at that door. They said, that has got to be an hour's line. They won't be giving us our table for two hours. We have to think of something else. That line's too long, what shall we do? Now, they could have said, let's say "excuse me but this is urgent." They could have said, could you part this crowd just a little bit, we got a paralyzed man coming through.

No, they said, it looks to me like we have got to take off the roof. We could get him in there, let's take off this roof. Let's just pull that roof off.

Now, what was a roof in the ancient Near East? First of all, there were some bearing beams. Then earthen matter. On top of that there was some grass that served as coolant, and then on top of all of that were some tiles. (The parallel accounts in Matthew and Luke talk about the tiles on the top of the roof.)

Well, this crowd, these "meek" four helpers who were going to help this paralyzed man, crawled on top of the roof. They rip up the tile, they throw away the hay. Who knows what the people in that crowd were thinking as tiles and hay are raining down on them. They're standing nicely in line and these four are up on that roof throwing down tiles, hay, and here comes the mud. Then they drag that poor paralyzed man on his mat. (Thankfully for us they don't give us the details of how that poor soul got up on the roof! Sometimes the redactor is kind and generous and doesn't tell us the details.)

Think of it. Think of yourself lying on a mat, thinking Oh, thank you, they're helping me now, I'm going to be well! And the next thing you know they're hauling you, mat and all, up to the roof and that isn't the half of it. The next thing you know you are coming down and doing so in the midst of a crowd that isn't all that happy to see you. You started out being paralyzed, now you've got bigger problems than that!

So, here he comes through the roof, coming down the other side in the midst of a crowd. Paralyzed man, mat, four friends and probably some leftover tiles, hay, and mud, all of it, in it comes.

Doesn't it figure that the scribes and Pharisees are in there taking notes? Well, they're going to write this one up! This Jesus is every bit as unconventional as they thought.

Jesus takes one look at this crowd, hay, tile, mud, mats, men and says, your faith, your confidence that you could get into this room, that he would be restored, your confidence that wholeness could be found for this man has taken away his affliction. In the ancient formula, "his sins are forgiven." That is, his brokenness is resolved. His wholeness restored. Because you have the confidence, you saw the line, and you said, we can't wait that long.

There's no time to wait on line. Ordinarily, we wouldn't jump line. Now, we can't even consider taking our turn. We have to get up on the roof and get in by whatever means takes us there. We can't wait in line to bring our children to health and wholeness.

Now, let's get back to these scribes and Pharisees. They've witnessed this whole breathtaking event and they rightly are going to take accounts. The scribes and Pharisees are the fellows who know the rules. They're the fellows who wrote the rules. In fact, sometimes they don't even bother telling us, the rest of us, what the rules are. But they always know what the rules are.

And this jumping in through roofs with paralyzed men is defi-
nitely not in the rule book. Worse yet, once this crowd, this unruly
crowd, got here, they started asking, who is this upstart rabbi to forgive sins? They know the rules. The rules are that only God forgives
sins. And by the way God doesn't even do that except at their direction. God tells them whose life is worth redeeming. They make a list,
or they say there's a means test, and they decide who can be saved
and who cannot be saved.

So, they're all upset about it and they talk among themselves.
Are you getting that down? You see that, he's forgiving sins, remember it. Five violations of forgiven sins, put it down.

Jesus just senses they're talking about him. They're not talking
to him, you understand. His spirit senses—I'll bet it just did. You
kind of know when someone's talking about you, don't you?

Jesus turns to them and says, in essence, what's the problem?
And they say to him, in essence, you're only a teacher. What are you
doing messing about in the healing and restoration of the people?
Don't you know we've got agencies for that, Health and Human
Services? We got divisions of children, youth, and family services.

Anyway, so they say, what are you doing messing about in a
healing? It's not your job.

In the Fairfax neighborhood of Cleveland, it's not the job of
churches to be healing people. That's for doctors and hospitals and
such. But my dear, dear friend, the Reverend Dr. Otis Moss Jr. and one
of his deacons thought that maybe the people couldn't stand in line and
get a different doctor every time and only have their symptoms treated.
They thought perhaps these children of God ought to see the same
doctor every time, and that the doctor ought to pray before he set
about his work, and patient and doctor ought to pray together, and
church and hospital should work together.

So, Dr. Otis Moss, after about seventeen years, worked to establish a hospital wing. In that good place, University Hospitals and
Mount Olivet Institutional Church are partners. Because when they
asked in Cleveland, who are you to heal? the answer was, We are
lovers of the whole soul of those who are ill. We are they who are willing to pull the tiles off your roof if need be. We are those who would
throw the hay aside and dig through the mud, and pell-mell we will
come through your roof and into your lap if need be. Because you got
some people here and they need to be whole.

I don't know if this is helping, but perhaps we're getting closer to understanding the efficacy of human agency. We have to be about our business. We need to be embraced by the constancy of God's love. We will never do this alone. We will never do this alone.

But we do it in the name of the Christ who still lives. If we have the courage and the faith and the discipline and, may I say, the humor to see us through, we can dare to plant our feet, look upon the brokenness of our society, and say, in the name of Jesus Christ, take up your bed and walk. You will be restored. We have the right to do that. But alas, only after we have clambered up on the roof, pulled off the tiles, thrown aside the hay, and dug through the mud.

Our friends will misunderstand. Oh, they say, that's an old 60s-style liberalism. It's going out of fashion. Oh, that's an old style of activism. Oh, in this day of high technology you could mount a more effective information campaign.

Do you think the problems we have are because we don't know enough? I mean, is that plausible? How much exactly do you need to know besides the fact that nearly thirteen million children are living in poverty in America every day, that nearly nine million children in this nation don't have health insurance?

Some will say, it's an old style, you got to be more focused, more strategic. The fact of the matter is we will not so much decide as discern. We will not so much calculate as consecrate. We will not so much evaluate as exalt. We will not copy the pattern of those around us—we will follow the pattern established by another.

Will the others misunderstand? Yes, they will. Knowing that we will be misunderstood, we remember that no matter where we go, if we ascend to heaven, God is there. If we descend to the sea, God is there.

Knowing even our friends may misunderstand, we repeat, "In the midst of tribulation, stand by me. When I do the best I can and my friends misunderstand, thou who never lost a battle, stand by me."

Discerning Our Calling

Our human agency ought *not* be confused with a frantic, impulsive hyperactivity, however well-meaning. Our efforts, our exercise of human agency, are a grace-filled response to God's love. It is our calling to the ministries and mission of child advocacy. It grows out of our sense that we are called by Christ himself to enable every child to live the life for which they were created. It is in service to the determination to live faithfully that we find ourselves drawn to the festering wounds of children's lives.

Recently, I have been struck again by the way in which the postresurrection stories of Christ so effectively integrate the theological teachings we have been discussing. In the last five or six years, my heart and my head have gone to those postresurrection stories again and again. Look with me, will you, at this one account in John, chapter 20.

> [19]When it was evening on that day, the first day of the week, and the doors of the house where the disciples had met were locked for fear of the Jews, Jesus came and stood among them and said, "Peace be with you." [20]After he said this, he showed them his hands and his side. Then the disciples rejoiced when they saw the Lord. [21]Jesus said to them again, "Peace be with you." (John 20:19–21)
>
> [24]But Thomas (who was called the Twin), one of the twelve, was not with them when Jesus came. [25]So the other disciples told him, "We have seen the Lord." But he said to them, "Unless I see the mark of the nails in his hands, and put my finger in the mark of the nails and my hand in his side, I will not believe."
>
> [26]A week later his disciples were again in the house, and Thomas was with them. Although the doors were shut, Jesus came and stood among them and said, "Peace be with you." [27]Then he said to Thomas, "Put your finger here and see my hands. Reach out your hand and put it in my side. Do not doubt but believe." [28]Thomas answered him, "My Lord and my God!" (John 20:24–28)

What do we make of this? What does this mean for us if we would be faithful? We know that the first Easter night the disciples were gathered in that room. The Gospel of John tells us that they were all there and they locked the door because they were afraid. They were afraid that they might actually have to follow the Christ, weren't they?

And it doesn't say how it happened that Jesus came among them. There's no account of them opening door. Nobody says they unlocked the door. It just says Jesus came and stood among them.

What were his words to them? His first words? "Peace be with you." Now, what might he have said? He might have said to them, where were you, my friends, when they came for me? Where were you when my mother stood alone at the foot of my cross? Why did you cut and run when I needed you the most? Why didn't you take up arms and try to help me? Why did you let me suffer? But none of that. His words are, "Peace be with you." His first greeting to them is "Peace be with you."

Think of how we might feel if we were there with the disciples. Astonished. Overjoyed. We can't even imagine, can we, the emotion in that room. We can't begin to know what that emotion was. But we are told in this account that they moved from fear to rejoicing. Interesting, isn't it, that it was only after those disciples present were shown his wounds that we are told they rejoiced to see their Lord.

Poor Thomas the twin has spent about two thousand years wandering through church history being known as "Doubting Thomas." He wasn't with the fellows that night. Who knows where Thomas was. That's an interesting story in itself. Maybe he went to George Street. Who knows?

Thomas is called "the doubter." Well, I want to rehabilitate Thomas here. I want to suggest that we should remember him as "Tactile Thomas," not Doubting Thomas, "Tactile Thomas." He said, "I won't believe it until I put my hands in the wound."

Well, we know that a week later, in that same place, they were gathered again and Thomas *was* with them, and Jesus appeared to them again. Jesus greeted them again in peace and Thomas in essence, asked the question. Remember the text. Thomas said, in essence, Lord, we knew you. We knew you in life and so we believe. But how will those who come after who never knew you—how will they have faith? How will they know? How will the people at Haley Farm know? How will the children of our cities know? How will the boys under the bridge in Brazil know? How will the hungry of the Sudan know? How will they know?

That's the context in which we have to hear Jesus' response to Thomas. He says, Thomas, if you want to have faith, and he says to each of us, if you want to have faith, then put your fingers in the wounds. Reach out. If you want to have faith, touch the place where the spear cruelly dug in or where the nails pierced hands and feet.

What a lesson in our day when men and women are pulled off the street corners with only the touch of latex gloves lest they be contaminated by touching the wounds. You want to have faith, says Jesus, touch the wounds. You want to have faith? Touch the wounds.

Children are wounded today. If you would have faith, sisters and brothers, touch the wounds. In the name of Jesus, touch the wounds of brokenness and misery; the wounds of neglect and abuse, personal and societal; the wounds of injustice, poverty, and bigotry. Touch the wounds and peace be with you.

From Dry Bones to a Living Movement for Children

I have always held back from this one text, because to my Presbyterian sensibilities, it seemed hyperbolic, too overdrawn, too bleak for the real circumstances.

This is the story of Ezekiel and the dry bones. Now, there is the problem of Ezekiel himself. You know, he is not quite a right person. Despite our wish to say nice things about the prophets, it must be acknowledged that Ezekiel is, as the kids say, out there.

Now, you know Ezekiel. He is the wildest and the woolliest of all the prophets. He is a Judean priest, the son of a Judean priest.

Ezekiel is a part of the brain drain. When Nebuchadnezzar decides there is trouble in the land and he is going to do away with those troublesome people, he doesn't start with the dull and ignorant. You don't have to get rid of the people that follow like sheep. But the smart ones who think about justice, you better get them out of Dodge if you mean to subdue the city.

So, Nebuchadnezzar says, you, Ezekiel, with them you go. And so off they go to Babylon.

Before the exile, Ezekiel's book is a wonderful book in the first twenty-four or twenty-five chapters. In his oracles of judgment that come before the exile, he says, look, we are not living right in this land. Big trouble is coming. And he takes out after the religious establishment of the orthodox Yahwehist theology.

The thing about Ezekiel is he gets under everybody's skin. He doesn't mind saying, yes, we are the chosen people of God and, yes, we are in a covenant, just as you all say. But you are acting like this is a patron God. You are acting like it is not a covenant, like it is a bonus and you have no responsibilities. And he rails at Israel and tells them, you are not living as the people of God. You are not living by the terms of your covenant.

And so they say, behind his back, that Ezekiel, he is starting to get on my nerves. That Ezekiel, he talks crazy.

Then the exile comes and Ezekiel, for the next ten books, rails at the enemy, which gives his own people a little bit of a breather.

And then they are in Babylon. You know, by the waters of Babylon, we sat down and we wept when we thought of Zion. He is in Babylon and then he offers his oracles of restoration.

This brings us to the story of the dry bones. Imagine, this is the happy talk of this book! Aren't you glad we skipped the oracles of judgment?

The valley of dry bones, the 37th chapter in the book of Ezekiel.

> The hand of the LORD came upon me, and he brought me out by the spirit of the LORD and set me down in the middle of the valley; it was full of bones. ²He led me all around them; there were very many lying in the valley, and they were very dry. ³He said to me, "Mortal, can these bones live?" I answered, "O Lord GOD, you know." ⁴Then [God] said to me, "Prophesy to these bones." Well, now, this is Ezekiel's favorite activity. Yes, indeed, I will.
>
> "And say to them: dry bones, hear the word of the LORD. ⁵Thus says the Lord GOD to these bones: I will cause breath to enter you, and you shall live. ⁶I will lay sinews on you, and will cause flesh to come upon you, and cover you with skin, and put breath in you, and you shall live; and you shall know that I am the LORD."
>
> [And Ezekiel says,] ⁷So I prophesied as I had been commanded; and as I prophesied, suddenly there was a noise, a rattling, and the bones came together, bone to bone. ⁸I looked, and there were sinews on them, and flesh had come upon them, and skin had covered them; but there was no breath in them. ⁹Then [God] said to me, "Prophesy to the breath, prophesy, mortal, and say to the breath: Thus said the Lord GOD: Come from the four winds, O breath, and breathe upon these slain, that they may live." ¹⁰I prophesied as he commanded me, and the breath came into them, and they lived, and stood on their feet, a vast multitude. (Ezekiel 37:1–10)

Now, as they say, go figure! How many of us know that song, "Dem Bones, Dem Bones?" It is a lot of fun singing it, especially if you can remember which bone is connected to which other bone.

Yet the happy lyrics and melody of "Dem Bones" masks the grim reality of Ezekiel's account of the valley of dry bones. Is this the grimmest moment for children we have known since the founding of the Children's Defense Fund? Is the faith-based movement for children now a valley of dry bones? In many ways it seems so. Millions of children in poverty, lacking health care, unable to attend the Head Start programs for which they are eligible.

Dry. Hope gone. A movement faltering because its hope is shaky, its prospects slim. Has the imperial Nebuchadnezzar broken our spirits and broken our backs? Have we been sent off into our own Babylonian captivity?

Now, we have seen bad times before. There was a time we hoped so much for a new young president and were betrayed by his welfare reform, and it broke our hearts and it broke our spirit for a time.

Can you imagine that valley of dry bones? We are not talking about recently deceased carcasses. We are talking about a people slain where they stood, denied a proper burial, broken by tax cuts, imprisoned by lack of services, betrayed by the promise of jobs, died right where they stood, and their bones bleached by the harsh and unforgiving sun.

The truth is we live in a season, in a time that is dominated by beautiful lies and ugly truths. It is a beautiful lie that tax cuts stimulate the economy and create jobs that employ people who can then feed their children and pay their health care insurance.

The ugly truth is the jobs are moving offshore, and forty-five million of our citizens lack health care insurance, and 80 percent of them work in jobs lacking benefits.

Beautiful lies and ugly truths. Beautiful lie: we have the best health care system the world has ever known. Beautiful lie. Ugly truth: nine million children are uninsured and aren't assured of care when they are sick, let alone preventive care.

Beautiful lie: we are spreading democracy and freedom all around the world. Ugly truth: our nation's stock has never been lower in the community of nations. We are gaining new enemies moment to moment and day to day. Abu Ghraib and Quantico are monuments to our determination to subvert democracy.

Beautiful lies, ugly truths. Beautiful lie: this is a land of equal opportunity. Ugly truth: some of our children receive the best of our nation's many blessings and some are denied, by family circumstances and societal indifference, the basic necessities of life.

Beautiful lie, ugly truth.

The Reverend Dr. Bill Coffin said this may be somebody's idea of a peaceable kingdom. You know, the peaceable kingdom, where the lion and the lamb lie down together. Yes. But the lamb is not getting much sleep.

The Babylonian captivity, the valley of dry bones is all about this time of beautiful lies and ugly truths. And it is not just because of the suffering we have just named. It is not just, as though that were not enough, the treachery and duplicity of public policy.

But for people of faith, there is a smugness that rivals the orthodox Yahwehist theologians of Nebuchadnezzar's era. Some dare to call all this "the society that is living out its Christian values." Now, there is a beautiful lie.

Well, like Ezekiel, Marian Wright Edelman has long been a prophet. Now, I must say, she is a far more socially acceptable person than Ezekiel. Ezekiel's got stories to tell and he's got a way of telling them that would make your hair curl.

But Ezekiel is speaking to us and for us as we look over the current valley of dry bones. His circumstances offer a lesson to us. Like Ezekiel, if we tell the truth, we are not going to be popular. If you want it to be easy and you want everybody to pat you on the back, you better get a new line of work, because even Dr. King looks best in the rearview mirror.

It wasn't a lot of fun in the face of those hoses and dogs, and did we mention a rifle sight. Oh, yes, in the rearview mirror it looks better. To be a contemporary prophet is to speak an uncomfortable word.

So, if you want them to look good, you want to step back and admire your work, get another line of work, because we are going to speak like Ezekiel.

We are going to speak about the covenant and its responsibilities, its human responsibilities. Not just God's. The covenant wasn't just about God loves us best, God is on our side. The line of David is assured. Jerusalem will always be our capitol. Those are the pillars of the Yahwehist theology.

Oh, the Yahwehists could be dismissive of all those other parts of the covenant, like "I will be your God and you will be my people and you will have no other God before me." All those things that are so inconvenient to recall.

We live in a difficult time, a time, may I say, of Babylonian captivity. In recent years the debate has raged about faith-based initiatives. Much of the debate has had a tone of mystical confidence in services offered by faith-based organizations. This mystical confidence continues even in the face of evidence to the contrary. A cynic might assume that behind all the high rhetoric lies a political aspiration to get all these service programs off the government's to-do list and make them, in the eyes of the public, the charitable responsibility of churches, synagogues, and mosques.

Well, I'm a social scientist and a historian by training. I don't know about the politics of it, but I do know, regarding the faith-based initiative, that what is good is not new and what is new is not good. Many programs, including Head Start, have long been housed in buildings owned by the faith community. These are old faith-based initiatives and many of them, including programs like soup kitchens and homeless shelters, are among the best and safest of their kind. Newer forays into faith-based efforts suggest churches and others might engage in such activities as job training. The *initiative* in such matters clearly lies within governmental agencies. Faith organizations are responding to governmental initiative (and proffered dollars) to carry out missions and ministries for which they may be ill equipped.

At the community level, pastors and lay leaders often know best whose heart is breaking and why. They know, too, how best they might work with others and who those others might be. Distant denominational structures, much less governmental agencies, are poor substitutes.

I serve as a Parish Associate at a wonderful Presbyterian Church in a small New Jersey town. One year, we decided we were going to have a Crop Walk, a walk to raise money to help people all around the world through Church World Service, the humanitarian aid agency of the National Council of Churches.

We made plans, all the clergy in town, to walk in the Crop Walk. One local pastor of a congregation of a large conservative denomination said, "Why don't we start at my church because I've got the biggest parking lot and it is the most central and we can walk from there."

So, we made all our plans and the day came that we were to go on our Crop Walk. But early that morning, this pastor, just a young fellow who had never been to seminary, called and said, "Reverend, it is terrible. My superintendent says I can't participate in the Crop Walk because you all are leftists. He is not sure you are Christians."

I said, "Just us, the Presbyterians, or does that go for the Lutherans and Methodists and Episcopalians, too?"

"Yeah," he said, "all of them."

How we revert to tribalism. It is me and my kind. He continued, "I can't do it. They will throw me out."

I said, "Well, of course, don't do that. We don't want you to risk your church, don't do that. But since everybody is coming there, can we still park our cars in your lot anyway?"

"Yeah," the young pastor responded, "he didn't say nothing about the parking lot. I guess you could go ahead and park."

We went and we assembled and we went on our Crop Walk. It's a fairly short walk and before long we returned to the parking lot.

When we came back, every single one of our cars had been washed and polished and a little note had been stuck under the windshield wiper blade saying, "We're sorry we couldn't walk with you, but we washed your cars, because we couldn't wash your feet."

I say he walked with us. What do you say? We cannot be cowed by those organizations. Just stand them right down. Can't you just hear the phone call? "No, superintendent, I didn't walk with them. No, sir. I didn't bear any witness. I let those leftists do it all themselves." Everybody there knew that God had been in that place. Now his was an authentic faith-based initiative.

In the valley of dry bones we must discern our calling based on the destruction before our eyes, not on the professed priorities of a distant bureaucracy. Now, we have lots of missives that come across our desks as pastors or Christian educators, child advocates. We don't have to listen to them all.

I have learned a lot of things in airports, because I am in airports a lot. I was going from New York to Denver to Vancouver last fall, and I got to Denver—and by the way, if you are going to Denver, the airport is in about Kansas. It is absolutely not anywhere near Denver, that is for darn sure. Well, I got there. I think they let me off in about Nebraska, and then my flight was going out of a gate in Kansas. So, I walked on over there.

I finally got to the waiting area by my gate, and I sat down next to a lady, an older lady. Before long, the flight attendant picked up the microphone by the gate door and did what they all do, you know, Welcome to Flight 783 or whatever. "In a moment, we will be boarding, and I have a special announcement for you." Her next words over the intercom were unintelligible through some static. As she sat down, we didn't have a notion of what she had said.

A few minutes later, she went back to the microphone and said, "This is an international flight. We will be crossing a border, and I want you to know that in order to cross the border, you will . . ." and then her words again became unintelligible.

Finally, she gave it another try, and I thought I got it that third time through. (I'm a mother, I can understand anything.)

The older lady seated next to me said, "Excuse me. I'm a little hard of hearing. Did you understand what she said?"

I said, "Well, not the first two times, but on that third time, I believe what she said was, 'If you checked in here at Denver, you need to have your passport available for the boarding agent; but if you boarded anywhere else, the people there at the start of your journey checked it and you can just put your passport away and go on.'"

Well, she thought about that for a moment trying to sort out what it meant. So, as a little clue, I asked, "Did you board here in Denver?"

"Yes," she said, "I live here in Denver."

I said, "I believe you need to show your passport."

We looked at our tickets and it turned out I was in 12-C and she was in 12-D. When it came time I helped her with her little bags, because she had to, of course, show her passport.

So, we got in the air after some time and they began giving all the announcements. She reached across the aisle and tapped me. "Miss," she said, "I'm a little hard of hearing, you know, and I really don't need to know what to do if this plane crashes, but if they say anything about white wine, would you give me a little wave?"

You know what? We don't have to listen to every word of our generation either, but if they say anything about cups of wine, you pay attention. If they say anything about bread broken, if they say anything about cups of wine poured out, you stand to attention.

I don't know if this plane is going to crash, but if it does, you don't need the instructions. But if they say anything about wine, listen.

Well, I'm thinking again about those dry bones. Let me go back to the end of the story.

The end of the story is that God restores them. This is an oracle of restoration. But it is not "shazam." It is not wizardry. It is the Lord who acts. The description is rather complete and it is a fourfold restoration.

First of all, the bones, all those scattered parts of the movement, will come together. The bones will be gathered up, bone upon bone, until it is not a bunch of disparate parts but an organic whole.

And then the Lord says, I will lay that sinew on bone, which I have knit together. Then I will lay on muscle. You know, the power to get things done. I am going to put some muscle on that bone.

And it is a dangerous world out there. So, after I put the bone upon bone with sinew and put the muscle on the bone, I am going to cover it all with skin to protect you.

But still, it is not a life. The skin is protecting and shielding, the muscles are giving you power, the sinew is making the organic whole, but then the spirit is going to animate you. We are going to breathe into your nostrils just like the dawn of creation.

And then it says, "And stood on their feet, as a vast multitude." Or in some versions, they rose up as a vast army.

The spirit animated them. The Lord put bone to bone, sinew to bone, muscle to bone, skin to cover it all, and breath into them, and they rose up and stood as a vast army, even in Nebuchadnezzar's imperial valley of captivity.

There are at least three observations we might make regarding the process of restoration in this oracle.

First, the restoration happens at God's initiative. It is the Lord of life who transforms bleached, dry bones into living, vital men and women. We hear in clearest terms of the omnipotence of God's capacity, a thematic strain present throughout the witness of scripture.

Second, restoration does not happen all at once but little by little. Bone to bone, sinew to bone, muscle to bone then finally the breath of life. Our expectations should not be for a sudden and complete reassembly of all that we have striven for but an incremental and progressive development of that which will allow our children to stand.

Finally, we observe that this restoration process is not individual but corporate. We will not be restored in isolation from one another. The race does not belong alone to the swift. In this valley of death and destruction we must all become well and whole together. Recall that one of the first precepts for how we do Bible study is to remember that this is a book that is primarily addressed to communities, not individuals.

Now, how can these things happen? A preacher tells a story about a chess champion. A chess champion went to an art gallery with a friend, and he wasn't much interested in the art, but he wanted to accompany his friend.

They walked through room after room. Finally, they came to a rather well-known Impressionist painting called "Checkmate." It was a picture of a chessboard and two players with a game in process. He's kind of interested. I mentioned he's a chess champion. He knows chess.

He said to his friend, "You go on and see the other rooms. I'm taken by this picture. I just want to stare at this."

Staring and staring. Two hours go by. The friend saw the rest of the museum and came back. Pretty soon, the guards said it was time to close up. They came along to this fellow, still standing and looking at that chess picture, "Checkmate."

So, the guard and the friend asked, "What has so occupied you here?"

He said, "That says checkmate. It's not a checkmate. The king has another move."

You hear what I'm saying. This is not a checkmate. Why? The King has another move. It is not a checkmate because the King has another move.

So take that to heart and be of good courage. Dem bones, Dem bones, Dem dry bones, they are going to live, they are going to be knit together, they are going to draw strength, they are going to have the spirit of the Lord, and they are going to stand on their feet as a mighty army, because the King, because the King of Kings, has another move.

CHAPTER FOUR

Where Are We?
Here I Am, Send Me:
A Theology of Leadership,
Christian Vocation,
and Missiology

This book of reflections has set forth an approach that would lead us to believe that any doctrine or teaching would have to meet the criteria of better expressing, whose we are, who we are, where we are, what time it is, and what just happened.

So, with that template or theological construct, we go ahead now and look for a specific doctrine or a theology of leadership, a theology of Christian vocation, and a missiology that answers the question, where are we? Recall with me that Moses' response to finding himself on holy ground was to say, Here I am. Send me.

The Vocation of Leadership

All who aspire to leadership must be reflective. There is always something new to learn and leadership is a changing reality. So, we make bold to listen to Scripture again and hear what words it would teach us of a theology of leadership.

Now, biblical literature is replete with stories of leadership. We have cheek-by-jowl leaders in this book, and they proceed through our minds and through our memories. Many of the narratives speak of various kinds of leadership. Taken together they offer to us a coherent vision of leadership. Many of the New Testament narratives bring us so briefly into contact with the characters that we aren't able to discern the whole of the vocation or the whole of the theology. But we've met many leaders there. That good Samaritan from a hated and betrayed race who stopped to help. Some fellows who clambered on top of a roof and pulled its tiles off, so determined were they to bring their friend into the presence of Jesus.

And all of these are acts of leadership. But they are incidents of leadership and not a whole vocation of leadership. For a whole vocation of leadership let's look at the first chapter of the book of Joshua and then two verses from chapter 24.

> After the death of Moses the servant of the LORD, the LORD spoke to Joshua son of Nun, Moses' assistant, saying, [2]"My servant Moses is dead. Now proceed to cross the Jordan, you and all this people, into the land that I am giving to them, to the Israelites. [3]Every place that the sole of your foot will tread upon I have given to you, as I promised to Moses. [4]From the wilderness and the Lebanon as far as the great river, the river Euphrates, all the land of the Hittites, to the Great Sea in the west shall be in your territory. [5]No one shall be able to stand against you all of the days of your life. As I was with Moses, so I will be with you; I will not fail you or forsake you. [6]Be strong and courageous; for you shall put this people in possession of the land that I swore to their ancestors to give them. [7]Only be strong and very courageous, being careful to act in accordance with all the law that my servant Moses commanded you; do not turn from it to the right hand or to the left, so that you may be successful wherever you go. [8]This book of the law shall not depart out of your mouth; you shall meditate on it day and night, so that you may be careful to act in accordance with all that is written in it. For then you shall make your way prosperous, and then you shall be successful. [9]I hereby command you: Be strong and courageous; do not be frightened or dismayed, for the LORD your God is with you wherever you go." (Joshua 24:1–9)

Now, this character Joshua is lodged in what's known as the Deuteronomic history. Deuteronomy, the book we know as Deuteronomy, is the introduction for the narrative that covers Joshua, Judges, first and second Samuel, and first and second Kings.

Joshua is that narrative account that tells the story. Moses is gone. Moses was the one that led the people out of Egypt and now he's gone. What is to become of us, the Israelites may well have asked.

And our God who raises up men and women in every generation said, "Still your heart. Joshua, come here. I have something I want to say to you."

And then in those nine verses we just read, the holy one of spirit, Yahweh, lays it out. This, God says, is the vocation of leadership. So, today, we listen to that text again and ask, in this third millennium, in this global community, in this atomized, mean-spirited weary world, what does it take to lead?

The first word I hear echo back is courage. Courage. Courage. Courage. Well, what in the world is courage? When I was a child, I was afraid of something. I don't remember what it was, it might have been dragons, might have been thunderstorms, might have been roller coasters, might have been my big brother. I don't remember what it was.

But someone said to me, "Eileen, you have to have courage."

I said, "What does that mean? Do I have any of it?" Well, courage is not the absence of fear, said this voice. Courage is the ability to go on in spite of your fears. Then I knew for sure I didn't have any. What does that mean? Going ahead anyway seems a lot like not having fear.

I pondered that for some time. And then I heard a different explanation in my seminary years, when someone said, Courage is fear that has said its prayers. Saying your prayers doesn't make fear go away, does it? Prayer doesn't even automatically make you go on in spite of the fear.

But when we pray, when we say we're not in this alone, when we say, "O Lord, share this burden," when we say, "Pick up my portion. I'm trembling," when we say, "I'm not certain. I'm afraid. I'm lost. I'm not sure where to go," then courage comes to us.

Because the voice of the Almighty says to us as Yahweh says to Joshua, It's all right, go ahead, be afraid. Doesn't God in essence say to Joshua, If I were in your place, I'd be afraid, too. But I am with you. God doesn't say it's not going to be scary. God just says we will be accompanied on the journey.

Now, what most of us know about Joshua is all that business about fitting the battle of Jericho. And most of us haven't got a clue what "fit" might mean in relation to Jericho and battles.

It is true the first six chapters of the book of Joshua are dedicated to the conquest of that land, crossing the Jordan, crossing that

Jordan into what was promised to you. Crossing Jordan and meeting armed resistance.

And, yes, indeed, Joshua shows us in those first six chapters that he is an astute military leader. More than that, he gives courage to his troops. He helps them to be bold. He sets them off in the right direction, he deploys them properly.

But we're very remiss if we stop there. The measure of Joshua's leadership—and I would suggest the measure of anyone's leadership—is not in the moment that they encounter armed resistance, but it is when they have taken a victory and it is theirs to establish the community thereafter.

Do you know what I'm saying? This is a subtle matter. The measure of leadership is not in how we encounter armed resistance alone but is also in how we comport ourselves when victory is ours.

Let's look at Joshua in that light. Joshua possesses the skills not only of a great military leader but those of a diplomat and a statesperson. In fact, combined in Joshua, we see all the styles of leadership.

Joshua is the first great consulter in the Bible. Joshua consults; he's all the time running off to consult with this one or that one. He's all the time gathering the information. How do you see this, sister? What is your thought, brother? How did you see yesterday's events, and where do you think we ought to be headed tomorrow?

And then Joshua takes those thoughts to his God. He says, God, this is what I heard, help me make sense of these views.

And then Joshua speaks a word of prophecy and priestly comfort. He says a word of direction. There's nothing indecisive about Joshua, is there? What with that battle fitting and so forth. Nothing indecisive. But there is something consultative and there is something derivative. Joshua counts on Yahweh. Joshua just doesn't set about making decisions. Joshua consults with Yahweh. Joshua works to build consensus and then he takes it all to the Lord in prayer.

Well, comes a time the Israelites cross that Jordan. They begin to make their community and as a people they look ahead and think, we have arrived! Maybe you've crossed the Jordan, too, some little rivulet that you gave the name Jordan. You said, and when I cross that one, I will be whole. When I get through that course of study, when I finish that job, when I get that promotion, when I convince that city council, when I get that bill through the Congress, I will have crossed into that land that was promised to me. I have arrived!

And then, after all, what need do we have of Yahweh once we stand on the other side of the Jordan? Yahweh was a transportation system. Gods get to be meddlesome when they hang about after they've delivered you into the promised land.

So, as people will, these Israelites take a look around. They're meeting the gods of the Amorites, people already there. I don't know too much about the gods of the Amorites, but it seems they drank a better vintage of wine. Maybe they had the houses on the hillside. Maybe they drove a better model of donkey.

They look about and they say, there's some nice features of this god of the Amorites. Maybe the god of the Amorites allows them to sleep in on Sunday mornings. Maybe they have worship at some nice convenient time, say, 2:30 Tuesday afternoon. Or maybe— maybe the preacher over at the Amorite church only preaches three or four minutes.

They look about and the Amorites have a kind of nice attractiveness to them. And these Israelites, long – long, long—the people of the God of Abraham, begin to say to one another, I take a fancy to that Amorite god, how about you? I've been thinking of changing my membership over to the Amorite church. I wouldn't change myself, but the wife likes the choir over to the Amorites. We'd never forsake Yahweh, but the children need the Sunday school and the Amorites have the best Sunday school in town.

Besides that, those Amorites seem to have a higher income than we do. They seem to be kind of a special people, get kind of a leg up in anything they want. And I'm wondering if I hang with the Amorites long enough, will they begin to think of me as one? Will it kind of rub off on me? Will people start to address me, "Good morning, Mr. Amorite," instead of "Hey you"?

And after all, I've got all the things that Yahweh has promised me. Yahweh promised us to come across the Jordan. So we have. And now I can scarcely remember those days out in the wilderness. Oh, and the memory of slavery, it's gone.

So, I thought I'd just move on up, get away from these people, shake the dust of Egypt off my feet and set out for Amorite land.

Well, Joshua could have waited for the coup d'etat that would surely come and sweep him from office. Joshua could have caught up those first people that wandered over to Amorite land, couldn't he? He could have said, where are the people that turned in their membership over at Amorite land? And he could have punished them severely and in front of all the others.

But that's not what Joshua decided to do. As we go along to about the middle of the book of Joshua, the eleventh and twelfth chapters, this Amorite thing is catching on. People are starting to move in droves. The name of Yahweh is hardly called any more. The memory of wilderness, of slavery, of the God who gave manna, and most especially of that law that was brought down off the holy mountain, has dissolved in the absence of struggle.

Where did we put that law? Well, it's here somewhere, even if we have to look it up. But it's kind of senseless to be walking around carrying it. I don't believe I need that law any more. I am safe and well on the promised side of the Jordan. Maybe that was really intended only as the law for the wilderness. Maybe it doesn't pertain to me any more.

Well, Joshua faced all this and he could have, maybe should have, brought about a bloodbath, calling the ones who had been disloyal. But instead he comes to a little town, a town hardly remembered in our hearts, a town called Shechem.

In fact, the archaeological site of Shechem was only discovered about eight years ago and is being excavated even now. At Shechem, well into the heartland of the promised land, Joshua gathers his people around.

And he says, "People," and this is leadership, "let us remember what just happened. Let's remember who we are and whose we are, where we are, what time it is, and what just happened." So Joshua brings the people together at Shechem and together they talk.

There at Shechem they begin to recall their history. Who was it that plucked Moses out of obscurity and made him our leader? Who was it that sustained us, gave us manna out in the wilderness? Who told us we were coming home one day? Who laid out a home for us? Who told Moses he should not live to see the promised land? Who took Moses home and then raised up Joshua?

And so it went. It was at Shechem then that the people remembered who they were and renewed their covenant with Yahweh. The covenant renewal ceremony is a central event in the history of the ancient Hebrews. It's when they decided anew that they would be

God's people. It's when they remembered that they were once no people at all, just random individuals, but their people-hood, their beloved community-ness, came out of their identity as Yahweh's people.

Then the tribes renew their covenant and with such beautiful words. Look and listen to this leadership in Joshua 24:

After this long recitation of the salvation history of the Hebrew people, Joshua says to that clan,

> 14"Now therefore revere the LORD, and serve him in sincerity and in faithfulness; put away the gods that your ancestors served. . . ."—now speaking of the Amorites.
> 15"Now if you are unwilling to serve the LORD, choose this day whom you will serve, whether the gods your ancestors served in the region beyond the River or the gods of the Amorites in whose land you are living; but . . ." says Joshua, . . . as for me and my household, we will serve the LORD." (Joshua 24:14–15)

As for me and my household, we will serve the Lord. Joshua says, you can sweep me out of office if you want. You can take my senate seat. I could lose the chairmanship of this committee. I might lose my pastorate. But, for me and my household, we will serve the Lord. You can make me some little unimportant soul, I won't be your Joshua any more, I'll just be some soul. But choose this day whom you will serve. As for me and my household, count on it, we will serve the Lord.

Well, I do believe this brings us to the theology of leadership. What does it mean? That's fine for Joshua. We always like these brave stories, don't we? Man, was that guy brave. Me? You're talking to me? Well, that's another matter, isn't it?

We need to lead. There isn't some other body out there. If there is to be a movement for the justice for children—and that, a harbinger of that great justice of the land we were promised, the realm and reign of God—if there is to be a beloved community, we must provide that leadership.

Not some other body. Just us. So, we will have to answer every day, who will you and your household serve? Will we consult with Yahweh? Will we take counsel with one another? Will we hold that which we think and believe and worry about up to God and prayer and say, "Take it God and us with it?" Lead and we will follow. And we will offer leadership to those who come behind.

Now, today in America, there's a great deal of confusion about leadership. You know, I am often on airplanes that don't take off on time. In fact, that's redundant. I'm often on airplanes, the rest is to be assumed.

Well, when you're on an airplane and you can't get to your briefcase, because it's in the overhead bin under seven suitcases, you read anything there is to read, especially if you're a Calvinist, desperate reader. And you can only read that safety card so many times. I want you to know if ever there's an emergency, I'm going to be aces with that window.

In the seat-back pocket in front of me, sometime this spring, was *Publisher's Weekly*. Now, for most that would be a boring thing to read. Remember, I'm a pastor. This is really entertaining literature compared with what we usually read.

So, I pulled out *Publisher's Weekly* and I was reading about the hot topics for book titles. Computers were on the list, not surprisingly. Various things about the Internet and computers are hot sellers. S-e-x is still doing very well. Quite a number of titles.

But in either third or fourth position were books about leadership. I thought, that's very interesting, and Joshua sprung to mind. I didn't see a single word about Joshua in those titles.

I saw things along the lines of, *The Twelve Secrets of Great Leaders; The Seven Other Secrets of Incredibly Successful People;* or, for those with a short attention span, *The Two Secrets of People Who Want Power Now.* If this is so effective, why is it so secret? I couldn't quite figure that out. Why do all these people who are such leaders have all these secrets?

The Bible isn't a very secret book, is it? Right there for anybody to read. No secrets. In fact, it's a story we most like to tell, isn't it, the salvation story of God. God's persistent attention to leading us into a promised land, into a kingdom of God or, as we sometimes say these days, a "kindom" of God, a place where all people are family.

Well, I began to read the little summaries of the twelve secrets, the seven secrets, and the two secrets. And I have two conclusions to report back to you.

One, there's a good reason they keep it secret because it dare not speak its name. As some young people of my acquaintance would say, the central secret is how to "get over" on somebody. How to get your way. How to put yourself first. How to make sure you get yours and the devil take the hindmost.

The other secret is it's not leadership, it's management. It's not leadership; it's management. How do I take this and put it over here and take that and put it over here and somehow convince all of you that I've changed things? How do I move this one and this one and this one so that the people who are limping, limp more quietly? How do I move this thing, put it over here and put this one in charge so that he no longer tells me his people are hungry? How do I give them this grant so they can spread some money around the community, give back a report that says things are much better, and it never touches the ones in want?

Maybe they *ought* to keep it secret. We certainly don't need more people learning about it.

Leadership, that's a different quality all together. It's about saying come on ahead, tell me where it hurts. We can't do anything unless we know. I need to consult with you and you and you. I need to know where hearts are breaking. I need to know where dreams are deferred and dreams are dying. I need to know where people can't even dream dreams any more because they can't get their sleep because the gunfire keeps them awake. The fear keeps them awake. The fright about tomorrow keeps them awake. There are no secrets of management that make that go away. There is only balm in Gilead and it doesn't have to do with managing.

Now, is there anything more maddening than being managed? I have often prayed for patience. I'm not a patient person. You know, God, give me patience, NOW! Well, I'm being tested in these days. I believe some of you have been praying that prayer, haven't you? Give me patience, NOW!

I am sure you've had the same experience I've had telephoning large organizations. The phone rings and a recorded voice says, "Our menu has recently changed. Please listen carefully." And then you commence. Even though you know you should hang up right then. But you get seduced. You go, maybe this time it will work. So, you listen to the menu and press that first button, whatever that button is supposed to be. Do you get a real live person ready to help you with whatever that topic was? No, you get another choice of buttons. Well, you've got the billing department. "If your bill was too much, press one now. If it was too little, press two now. If you're hoping to pay it in some currency other than U.S. dollars, press three now. If none of these suit your need, press star." Now, NEVER do that. Because that's going to take you right back to the menu.

Automated telephone systems seem to me to be the embodiment of poor leadership. They give instruction without interpretation or passion. In a remote voice they give the impression that they can lead you to the promised land. Yet when you follow their directions you find yourself back where you started. This is not leadership.

Leadership is imbued with other qualities that inspire, cajole, raise the level of debate, and respect the dignity of those who are to follow. There are still examples of leaders in our lifetime and in our daily lives whom we might heed.

On a tired day in Montgomery, Miss Rosa Parks exercised leadership and took a stand by sitting down. Not with flamboyant gestures but in quiet dignity, this sister changed America and she did it sitting down. Leadership acts on conscience.

Dr. King is celebrated for his physical courage and his eloquence of speech within the Freedom Movement. Those in the Vietnam era antiwar movement valued him as well for his constancy and generosity. Even when his close advisors counseled him not to oppose the Vietnam war and risk diluting his leadership and focus on Civil Rights, he followed his own conscience. The escalating war was wrong and misguided. In faithfulness to this belief he took the pulpit at New York's Riverside Church and said so. This act of generosity and moral courage gave strength to another cause that sought the common good. Leadership is generous.

Leadership isn't always wise. I have a member of my family, my sister, who is, as the world reckons, not a leader. She's mentally retarded and physically handicapped. She is nevertheless my only sister. She is my true sister and my dear sister.

Her sister (me) has a very expensive and complicated education, which is not to say she is smart. Beth Ann is retarded, which is not to say she is dumb. Beth Ann is, at some level, aware of the great discrepancy in our educational backgrounds, but she is not intimidated by it.

Some time ago, my mother celebrated her eightieth birthday. And as part of that weekend, we were on a ride out in the country, as my mother loves to do of an afternoon. I don't know, I haven't gotten to that age of motherhood. Apparently there comes an age when what you want to do is be taken on a ride out in the country. I guess I'm looking forward to that.

As we drove through a little park on a bright, sunny June day, we paused and watched the Hudson River, the people reading newspapers, and the children at play. My mother is attentive to all things, and she soon pointed out a large dog trotting with its owner. It was one of those dogs, really fancy dogs, with pointed ears and a white tail that curls, a beautiful white coat. I said, "What kind of dog is that, Mom? Is that an Aleutian or Samoyed or Husky? What do they call that kind of dog?"

From the back seat, Beth Ann confidently said, "That be a white dog." She may have an unfortunate diagnosis, but her self-esteem is intact, my sister. Leadership is confident. Leadership is not always rational. It's certainly not always well-educated. Sometimes it's just brave and confident.

Leadership always embodies the deepest values of the community. Leadership always draws from the deepest values of the community.

We have other examples of leadership around us. Think of Christopher Reeve. He was the fellow who played Superman in the movies and I, for one, missed that film. I didn't know who Christopher Reeve was. Then he fell off a horse, broke his neck, and became a paraplegic. He caught my attention when he converted a personal agony into a public advocacy. And then I began to wonder if he wasn't Superman all along.

He took the agony of his stilled arms and legs, the crushed dreams of his film career, and he decided to take all that he had left to him and to place it in trust, to be a spokesperson for spinal cord injuries.

He took a personal agony. He made it a public advocacy. Help did not come in time for him. But help will come in time for someone because of him.

Leadership is forgiving. Leadership always gives another chance. There are many examples, but the most spectacular of our generation it seems to me is Nelson Mandela. He was at the Riverside Church shortly after his release, and he said, "Well, I never said I was in prison for something I didn't do. I did it. I believed in freedom." Remember what they predicted for South Africa? If apartheid falls, there will be a blood bath. Every white Afrikaner will die. So, even though it's got some shortcomings—easy for them to say, right?—

even though it's got some shortcomings, and it's a dirty little system, it's our system.

Well, God would not let apartheid have the last word. And Nelson Mandela stepped out of a prison and led his nation's transition to freedom. Leadership is forgiving and gives another chance.

The Church has always been the crucible for leadership. Our good friend and brother, Andrew Young, in his book *An Easy Burden*, tells a wonderful story in which he went to the United Nations as the U.S. Ambassador. The evening came when he was to present his credentials as the first African-American Ambassador to the United Nations. He had to fight to the finish with the studs in his tuxedo to get himself ready. But then he went across the street into that great assembly hall, presented his credentials, and spent the evening meeting people. At the end of the evening he went back and had the same fight to get out of that tuxedo. At last he sat down, had a cup of tea, and counted eleven heads of state or ambassadors with whom he was personally acquainted because of his work in the World Student Christian Federation decades earlier.

There was a day in America when we invested in our young people. There was a day in America when you couldn't move in a church on a Sunday night because of youth groups. And there was Westminster Fellowship and all those young people's groups. Every denomination had one.

Today there are fewer opportunities for our young people to learn leadership. The Ecumenical Institute of Bossey in Céligny, Switzerland, is one of the few remaining places where the brightest and best of a new generation get to know each other in a way that can only be done on that precious piece of holy ground in Céligny. And it will be another half century before the benefits are fully reaped by this world.

We must reinvest in leadership. We must once again serve as mentors and friends to the young. We must become leaders of the sort who are brave, not because they have no fears but because they have said their prayers. Conscientious, generous, confident, and thoughtful leaders.

Your grandmother probably told you the last important principle of leadership and somehow this message, this very simple message, is often lost. "Lead by example," she said. "By example," she said, "you lead."

So, these are some of the lessons of leadership. You may say to yourself, not me, I can't be all that. Heed Joshua and take the first step, choose this day whom you will serve.

Maybe you can't preach like Peter, maybe you can't pray like Paul, but you can tell the world of Jesus and say, he died for all. He will bring us into the promised land where it is not the color of skin or zip code or immigration status or even the content of character by which our children are judged by the Lord of the universe, but instead, by their blessed created-ness.

In Romans, Chapter 12, Paul, who never was one for summarizing anything, summarized these characteristics of leadership.

> I appeal to you therefore, brothers and sisters, by the mercies of God, to present your bodies as a living sacrifice, holy and acceptable to God, which is your spiritual worship. [2]Do not be conformed to this world, or the world of the Amorites, but be transformed by the renewing of your minds, so that you may discern what is the will of God—what is good and acceptable and perfect.
>
> [9]Let love be genuine; hate what is evil, hold fast to what is good; [10]love one another with mutual affection; outdo one another in showing honor. [11]Do not lag in zeal, be ardent in spirit, serve the Lord. [12]Rejoice in hope, be patient in suffering, persevere in prayer. [13]Contribute to the needs of the saints; extend hospitality to strangers.
>
> [14]Bless those who persecute you; bless and do not curse them. [15]Rejoice with those who rejoice, weep with those who weep. [16]Live in harmony with one another; do not be haughty, but associate with the lowly; do not claim to be wiser than you are. [17]Do not repay anyone evil for evil, but take thought for what is noble in the sight of all, . . . [21]Do not be overcome by evil, but overcome evil with good.

To summarize Paul: Lead when the spirit says lead. Lead when the spirit says lead. And choose this day whom you will serve. As for me and my household, we will serve the Lord.

Missiology

To what end do we seek such leadership among ourselves and others? How will the children's movement sustain the energy and focus to express our calling in a complex society in a postmodern world? Let us repair again to the prophet Isaiah, Chapter 40.

12Who has measured the waters in the hollow of his hand and marked off the heavens with a span, enclosed the dust of the earth in a measure, and weighed the mountains in scales and the hills in a balance?
13Who has directed the spirit of the Lord, or as his counselor has instructed him?
14Whom did he consult for his enlightenment, and who taught him the path of justice? . . .
17All the nations are as nothing before him; they are accounted by him as less than nothing and emptiness.
28Have you not known? Have you not heard? The LORD is the everlasting God, the Creator of the ends of the earth. He does not faint or grow weary; his understanding is unsearchable.
29He gives power to the faint, and strengthens the powerless.
30Even youths will faint and be weary, and the young will fall exhausted; 31but those who wait for the LORD shall renew their strength, they shall mount up with wings like eagles, they shall run and not be weary, they shall walk and not faint.

"They shall mount up with wings like eagles, they shall run and not be weary. They shall walk and not faint." In these reflections we've been pursuing the goal of a usable theology to undergird child-advocacy ministry. We have talked about the nature of holding some coherence in our beliefs, practices, prayers, and faithfulness to God. And we have just considered the vocation of leadership. Now we consider missiology. What are our theological ideas about our mission in the world? Or another way to say it, what does God intend for us to think about our mission? Or, when we think about God, what do we understand our mission to be? What are our missiological considerations? If there is a stumbling block over which the church has stubbed its toe these two thousand years, it has been this very one. What is our mission, what are we to be, and how are we to be that in fidelity and truth?

I can hardly think that a two-thousand-year-old dilemma is going to get resolved here and now, but if the Lord be kind and generous, at least we will find some discernment to this difficult question of missiology.

Missiology has at least two important touchstones in Christian thought. It is not just the question of *what* are we to do to be faithful, though that is its central focus, but also *how* are we to do what we are to do. Is it mission's goals or mission's means that matter? As long as we achieve our goals, does it matter how we get there?

So, these are two aspects of missiology: what are we to do to be faithful; and, how are we to do it to be faithful. This implied missiological tension has been a source of division in the church from the first Easter morning until this day. This missiological tension has expressed itself in two distinct tendencies.

One tendency says the Great Commission is the answer to the missiological question. We are to go to the ends of the earth and make disciples, that every knee shall bow and every tongue confess that Jesus Christ is Lord. To the very ends of the earth, they say, that is the essence of the missiological teaching. In this view the proclamation of Jesus as Christ is both the goal and means of mission.

Then there are others who emphasize the means of mission as derived from the commandment to love thy neighbor. The great missiological end, then, is to treat every human heart as if it were breaking. The great missiological end is to so be in the world as to show the love of God that is in Jesus Christ.

God forgive us, with these two wonderful sentiments the church has fought itself into hundreds of divisive denominational families over the last two thousand years.

With these two great commands, it hardly seems possible. Yet in our day the battle rages. It has a particular political permutation in North America, which we call the religious right and the religious left. Neither seems to have remembered that great priestly prayer of Christ in his last hours. Lord make them one, that the world might believe. Make them one people that the world might believe. One wag has observed that Christians have divided themselves into those who only picket and those who only pray.

These matters, these theological matters, are time-bound. Every generation must ask for itself, what does it mean today? Every generation of Christian must ask for themselves, what time is it, *¿Qué hora es?* What does our contextual situation teach us in terms of mission goals and means?

The great hymn of James Russell Lowell teaches us that "New occasions teach new duties. Time makes ancient good uncouth." Time makes ancient good uncouth.

Now, how does that work? How is it that something can be good yesterday and uncouth today? Ours is a spiritual journey. You don't stay in the same environment. You're moving across time and space. In each locale and each moment, faithfulness in mission must be weighed.

As we have noted earlier, a central aspect of our self-understanding is that the Church is called to be the body of Christ. The Church is to be Christ's body on earth. We are to be the Christ. Not just tell the story, but be the story. Yet even with this clear concept the Church's mission and means are not automatic.

Do we remember what happened to that body? Do we remember what happened to that body? It was pierced. It was disrobed. It was whipped and it was nailed. And it was hung in public ridicule. Then it was taken down and put in a borrowed cave. There the body languished three dark days until some women came along and said, "He's not here. He's not here." And then the glad proclamation came. "He lives."

Well, what can we surmise about the mission of a church that is to be the body of Christ? At least this: that we are to live as people who know they are one day going to die and perhaps not neatly.

We are to live as a people who know that they will one day perish and perhaps not tidily. And then, dear friends, we are to die as a people who know they will one day live.

That's what it means to be Christ's body, to live knowing we're going to die and then to die knowing we're going to live. The great vocation of the Church, to be the body of Christ.

Earlier I talked about the difference between leadership and management. In those books, about the seven secrets of the truly effective and the really precious secrets of the incredibly powerful, and all those books, the authors all extol the praises of a mission statement.

Well, I don't have any idea what they mean by mission statement. I think they mean a "to-do" list. Now, what's the difference, you say, between a mission statement and a to-do list? Well, I think there's a world of difference.

Your to-do list is what you do, the priorities you have for yourself this day. It's what you want to do, accomplish, be, see, acquire, or attain.

A mission statement implies a covenant with somebody else. A to-do list is just my priorities for me, where I'm headed today, what I want to do and get. A mission statement for the Church tells us where we are headed together. In short, there is a world of difference between a to-do list and a mission statement. A to-do list is a solitary enterprise. A mission statement embraces the whole of the world.

I'm very fond of the American theological writer Parker Palmer. And he tells a wonderful story of being in an airplane. They do all the things that they do before takeoff, and then they pull away and roll to one of those remote corners of the airport. His story of what follows invites us to embellish the account.

You know what that's like. You've been on those planes. And the pilot—I mean, only somebody who's behind a locked door could speak this calmly—announces, "Well, you know, we got some bad news for you. And then we got some worse news for you. The bad news is this: The town to which we are flying is all socked in and we've looked at all the alternatives and there aren't any. The worse news is they didn't get to put the food on the plane while we were back at the terminal. And now there's another plane in our parking space, so we're going to be sitting here for a few hours. Thank you for flying with us." Flying?!

Then the man behind the locked door says, "We here on the flight deck will keep in touch with you."

Well, in Parker Palmer's recollection, all you-know-what breaks out. Again, our own many similar experiences help us see and imagine the characters on board and their conduct. My personal favorite is the fellow in the three-piece suit who throws himself a little temper tantrum right there. You know that fellow? He's an important man. I don't know what the rest of us are, but he's important. Somebody's waiting on him.

He has a to-do list to beat the band. His is a two-volume work. And so he stands up and he pulls out his briefcase, which is on the bottom of seven cases in the overhead bin. He whips open that briefcase, he flops it on the seat, so we all know exactly how upset he is. He throws it down, he gets out his cell phone and his computer and his notebook. People in the aisle are ducking and bending.

Then there's the poor lady who gets hit with all the flotsam and jetsam from the overhead bin. You know her, too. She says, "Well, I never. I never." Then there's always somebody who selects this moment to say, "I don't feel so good." Somebody pinned on the other side saying, "Can I go to the bathroom?"

Well, this is a mess. This makes Noah's Ark look like a walk in the park.

The flight attendant, who of course does not have the luxury of being locked behind the door on the flight deck, gets on the PA system. She's like that dove. They send her out. Now, I don't know if this is an apocryphal story or if it happened, I just know Parker Palmer provides the outline of a story and our imaginations fill in the details. Anyway this poor woman, she's out there so, she gets on the PA system and she says something like, "I know it's very discouraging." More thumping, slamming, foot stamping. "And I know it's lunchtime and some of you want to eat. Some of you for medical reasons need to eat. Some of you probably shouldn't be eating anything. But you are a touch thirsty.

"Some of you have reading material, enough to go around. Others of you for the short flight have not brought anything. We have some breadbaskets left here from the last meal. I'm going to pass them down one side of the plane and back up the other.

"And I invite you to place in it whatever you can spare, might be a Lifesaver, might be that little sack of peanuts that's been in your purse since about seven. Could be the mints you pinched from the hotel this morning. Maybe you have some cheese and crackers, maybe a little bottle of water, maybe you just read a good article in a magazine, you could put it in there for somebody who has nothing to read.

"Some of you have some Rolaids. Some of you have a little Tylenol. Whatever you have that you can spare, put it in there."

She puts the breadbaskets down on those bulkhead seats—those people who were already in trouble with everybody else on the plane because they have some place to put their legs—and they begin to pass the baskets around.

Well, something takes place in that airplane. Suddenly purses are opening. Magazines are getting ripped, people are reaching in pockets, even you-know-who is up again. And up there where his briefcase was, he has a box of fine chocolates. And inspired by that, his seatmate gets up and finds a bottle of wine—well, it was water, but in these circumstances . . .

Pretty soon these baskets are full to overflowing and are passed about. And they come back up to the flight attendant. "Now," she says, "we're going to reverse the process. I'm going to start these baskets back down the aisles and you take what you need.

"If, for medical reasons, you need some protein, you take those peanuts. If your throat's a little dry and you need something to drink or you just enjoy a chocolate or a mint or you spot an article that looks good or an aspirin that might relieve a headache, help yourself."

Well, people are now in a festive mood. You've seen this overtake a plane. Now people are sharing. You need to get out to go to the washroom? How are you feeling? Some Rolaids here, would they help you? Madam, I heard you say you needed your lunch, there are some good things here.

Well, presently, all this gets done and finally the airplane rolls out of the remote corner, they take off, and in a short time are in that city they could have walked to in half the time.

As they're getting off the plane, Parker Palmer stops and says to the young woman, "You know there's a story like that in the Bible."

She says, "I know. That's where I got the idea."

It makes us think again, doesn't it? We remember that feeding of the multitude and we think again that maybe it wasn't a story about a catering service. Maybe it wasn't about food at all. It certainly wasn't about food in the airplane. It was about turning an angry, individualized mob into a community seeking the common good. It was about getting a bunch of people having temper tantrums and throwing briefcases up off their resources and sharing with others and focusing on the needs of the people around them. It was, for that moment, the recognition that they were hermetically sealed inside a single vehicle, and the fate of one was the fate of all. It wasn't even in the first or second instance about food. It was about learning how to enjoy what we have, sharing among ourselves. It was about enjoying each other's company, of coming to see what you carry in that briefcase, coming to see what treasures you have tucked away there. Coming to see what article you've picked out for me to read.

It was for spending our time pondering together our future, what would happen next. It was about being together and knowing we were going to be together and saying what do you think will happen, how are we going to live this thing out? This was a story about digging deep. I think it was about knowing we're in it together. I think it was about risking what you have, to get what you might need.

Well, it's a kind of missiological story, and it tells us about the importance of seeking after the common good. Not our good or my good or the good of the people sitting in the aisle seats or the good of the folk over here at the windows, but recognizing in life's great airplane, there's only one class of seating, and we're all in it together.

In every generation, this question needs to be asked and no one asks it better about our era, it seems to me, than Cornel West. One of the wonderful books he wrote is called Race Matters. His is a rare missiological essay with so much to teach us that I share it at length.

What is to be done? How do we capture a new spirit and vision to meet the challenges of the post-industrial city, post-modern culture, and post-party politics?

First, we must admit that the most valuable sources for help, hope, and power consist of ourselves and our common history. As in the ages of Lincoln, Roosevelt, and King, we must look to new frameworks and languages to understand our multi-layered crisis and overcome our deep malaise.

Second, we must focus our attention on the public square—the common good that undergirds our national and global destinies. The vitality of any public square ultimately depends on how much we care about the quality of our lives together. The neglect of our public infrastructure . . . reflects not only our myopic economic policies, which impede productivity, but also the low priority we place on our common life.

The tragic plight of our children clearly reveals our deep disregard for public well-being. About one out of every five children in this country lives in poverty, including one out of every two black children and two out of every five Hispanic children. Most of our children—neglected by overburdened parents and bombarded by the market values of profit-hungry corporations—are ill-equipped to live lives of spiritual and cultural quality. Faced with these facts, how do we expect ever to constitute a vibrant society?

One essential step is some form of large-scale public intervention to ensure access to basic social goods—housing, food, health care, education, child care, and jobs.[1]

Read that one again; I think we're getting very close to the heart of a missiological imperative. "One essential step is some form of large-scale public intervention to ensure access to basic social goods—housing, food, health care, education, child care, and jobs."[2] Cornel West continues,

We must invigorate the common good with a mixture of government, business, and labor that does not follow any existing blueprint. After a period in which the private sphere has been sacralized and the public square gutted, the temptation is to make a fetish of the public square. We need to resist such dogmatic swings.

Last, the major challenge is to meet the need to generate new leadership. . . . Only a visionary leadership that can motivate "the better angels of our nature," as Lincoln said, and activate possibilities for a freer, more efficient, and stable America—only that leadership deserves cultivation and support.[3]

We've almost come full circle, haven't we? Here we are talking again about leadership. So, let us listen for God's word to us in the 11th and 12th Chapters of Hebrews. We started this sojourn together, you and I, with Moses. Beginning with the 23rd verse:

[23]By faith Moses was hidden by his parents for three months after his birth, because they saw that the child was beautiful; and they were not afraid of the king's edict. [24]By faith Moses, when he was grown up, refused to be called a son of Pharaoh's daughter, [25]choosing rather to share ill-treatment with the people of God. . . . [27]By faith he left Egypt, unafraid of the king's anger; . . . [28]By faith he kept the Passover. . . . [29]By faith the people passed through the Red Sea as if it were dry. . . .

By faith, they lived on and entered a new land.

And then in Hebrews, Paul, having recounted those who lived by faith and where it took them, says, [32]*And what more should I say?*

For time would fail me to tell of Gideon, Barak, Samson, Fannie Lou, Martin, Desmond, and all those whose faith conquered kingdoms, administered justice, obtained promises, shut the mouths of lions, and quenched the raging fire.

[35]Women received their dead by resurrection. Others were tortured, refusing to accept release, in order to obtain a better resurrection. [36]Others suffered mocking and flogging, . . . [37]They were stoned to death, they were sawn in two, they were killed by the sword; they went about in skins of sheep and goats, destitute, persecuted, tormented. . . . They wandered in deserts and mountains, and in caves and holes in the ground. [39]Yet all these, though they were commended for their faith, did not receive what was promised.

They walked for another generation.

Therefore, since we are surrounded by so great a cloud of witnesses, . . . let us run with perseverance the race that is set before us, [2]looking to Jesus the pioneer and perfecter of our faith, . . . [12]Therefore lift your drooping hands and strengthen your weak knees, [13]and make straight paths for your feet, so that what is lame may not be put out of joint, but rather be healed. (Hebrews 12)

Missiology. Both the goal and the means count. We must proclaim Christ in both word and deed. Let us run with perseverance, taking this whole complex salvation history to heart. We may not see in this life what we were promised, but we will run and not grow faint. We will find ourselves borne up in the worst moment of our lives as if on eagle wings. And we will walk for generations yet unborn. Now, there's a missiology construct.

The wonderful Maryknoll missioners who have walked into the jaws of hell across this world for the love of God have a mission charge from their founder. I share it with you. Nay, I commend it to you. Nay, I charge you with it. "You go, you go where you are not wanted, but you are needed. And you stay there until you're wanted, but not needed." You go where you are not wanted, but you are needed. And dearly beloved, you stay there until you're wanted, but no longer needed.

In our mission context, can we do less? When all about us in this nation children are struggling and suffering, in desperate need of caring, committed adults who will go where they are needed—even if not always wanted—let us be the ones who are alert and conscious, who answer the question, where are you? with the sure response, here I am. Send me.

Notes

1. Cornel West, *Race Matters* (New York: Vintage Books, 1994), 11–12.
2. Ibid., 12.
3. Ibid., 12–13.

CHAPTER FIVE

What Time Is It?

Children and Child Advocacy
in Church History

We turn now to considering the Church's history, its theology, and how it informs us as child advocates. If we as a Church are to be alert and conscious, to answer the question, what time is it? we need to know where the Church stands in two thousand years of ministry to and with children. Having looked back at our history, we will have a better sense of what time it is for the Church right now. I will suggest that it is time for the Church to be a sanctuary for children, it is the hour for freedom. But before we look ahead, we look back.

What is the place of child advocacy within the ministry of the Church? Where does child advocacy fit in fidelity and faithfulness to the gospel of the Christ who still lives?

Where is it? Straight in the center of Jesus' heart. The only sanction in all of the New Testament, the only occurrence of our Lord saying, if you don't do this then that which will follow is found in Matthew 18: It is better for you to have a millstone hung about your neck, be dropped in the sea at its deepest part, than to cause one of these little ones to stumble.

So, what is child advocacy? Child advocacy is, quite simply, the ministry of removing stumbling blocks. We are the dear ones' stone masons. We are they who remove the clutter from around the feet of children, and the Church knew this from the very first.

The history of the Church is replete with debates about the inborn nature of the child, about human depravity and a sinful nature. Yet, even within the most adamant of such views is the theological argument for the created goodness of both Creator and creature. Moreover, a recognition that children are created in God's image contributes to a positive validation of what it means to be human.

The early Church knew, and even wrote, that children are to live the lives for which they were created. Think of it. What is the responsibility of the Church to the child? To see to it that the child lives the life for which he or she was created.

It doesn't say anything about making that child a good Methodist. It doesn't say he has to be Presbyterian (though it's not a bad idea.) Or Baptist. It doesn't say any of that, does it? Live the life for which he or she was created, and that's the deadly menace of our society. It's not that every child fails to have a Nintendo. It's not that they didn't all go to the Hamptons for the summer. It's not that they're not even going to get a glimpse of the Vineyard in August. They never got a chance. They never got a chance to live the life for which God created them.

So, from the very first, in the early days, the early centuries, the very first traditional practice of the Church with specific children is christening, the anointing with oil, the giving to the child his or her name. The very first child-specific practice of the Church is to take the child in arms, to take the oil from the olive tree, to anoint the child with the sign of the cross, and to say to the child, "You are," and then the child's name, "by the grace of God, you are," and say the child's name. The child of God by the grace of God.

How well has the Church maintained this tradition in the world that knows not the Lord? To anoint with oil every child and say to that child, by the grace of God you are Matthew or Malcolm or Cynthia, Donna or Deborah, by the grace of God you come and dwell among us. What of the children whose own families for whatever reason have neglected a tradition of faith? Does society not bear a responsibility to "anoint" them with the blessings of identity and welcome?

Christening from its earlier days had two functions. One was the function of the priest in anointing with oil, announcing the child's name. The second part was just as important. From the second century on, the Christian community anointed children with oil, called them by name for the first time, and then as a community made promises to lead the child by prayer and example. Now some of our churches practice infant baptism and others practice a ritual of dedication of infants and believers' baptism. But what of all the children to whom no religious or secular promise is made? Can it be that the Creator of all has no interest in such children? Can it be that the commonweal has no claim to celebrate the life of children beyond its membership? Are we reduced to the notion that children are the private chattel of their parents? I don't think so.

I believe that as a culture and a people we must lay claim to all children—not in the religious sense of claiming them for Christ, but as fellow human travelers we need to claim them. We need to say culturally, "This child doesn't belong to you, though you are the daddy or the mommy. This child is a blessing to all of us, so when the question is asked, 'Who will guide this child by prayer and by example,' the answer is, 'We will.'"

So, I ask you now for all our children, "Who will be there for those children and who by prayer and by example will nurture them?" I ask you in the confidence that your response will be, "We will." Did I hear that?

That they might live the lives for which they were created. Who will? We will. You know these children, don't you? No one's anointing them. No one's standing up for them. No one's there to say, we will. No one's there to pray for them and with them.

When I was growing up, we had something called a prayer reminder. Now, I never figured you needed one of those and a mother. You know what I'm saying. But some time around the late 1950s we had a little card that we hung on the wall that had a little white plastic cross and somehow that thing glowed in the dark. Probably was asbestos. Uranium or something. And when the lights went out, long after your mother had said, say your prayers, and long after you had, this little cross would glow in the dark.

I went through a period of time when I had a love affair with the Nancy Drew novels. And I used my flashlight to read at night. My mother would call out, "Do I see a light in there?"

"Must be the prayer reminder, Mother."

"I hope that's not a flashlight in there."

"Could be that prayer reminder."

Who's reminding our children today? We can't make enough of those crosses. Who's reminding children today?

In the Middle Ages, the Church through holy orders, monasteries, and convents became a refuge for homeless children. During Europe's plagues, there were many homeless children. And many of them became important and noteworthy theologians, monks, prophets, and teachers.

Now, the Church in the West drifted toward Christian education, partly because Western culture was drifting toward an almost salvational confidence in education. The Reformation and the Enlightenment elevated our gratitude for and response to rational faculty. For the last four hundred years or so, many of our traditions have been concerned with education, sometimes at the expense of spiritual formation.

The Church in the East, the Byzantine church, which did not experience the Enlightenment and Reformation of Western culture, was more apt to incorporate children in all the aspects of worship. In Orthodox churches you'll see very young children in the liturgy. There's often no indestructible educational wing for them to go to. There's no Sunday school teacher to get them out during the second hymn. While there are many children's programs in Orthodox churches, I believe they may do a bit better in enfolding their children in the Church community from the first.

Now, I grew up almost literally within the church, a preacher's kid. I always believed you could do almost anything you wanted over in the educational wing, because God was occupied over in the sanctuary. I figured there was a certain liberty associated with the educational wing.

The Church in the East, from the very first, distributed blessed bread to all. Not just to baptized adults, but to all. This, they said, is the bread of life. Who were they to withhold it from any? So, children participated in the Eucharist. Within Protestantism we have a mixed picture on extending this sacrament and its blessings to children.

My point is not to rehash the struggles over Eucharistic theology but rather to suggest that child advocacy is needed within the Church as well as without. Our children do not always entirely comprehend our rituals.

I learned this in an embarrassing way. When one of my sons was about five years old there came a rainy day, one of those days young mothers dread at their dawning. Sheets and sheets and sheets of rain with no letup in sight.

We told stories and sang songs and made puzzles, baked cookies, planned dinner, and then at 9 a.m. we tried to find something else to do. By noon I cracked under pressure. Against every instinct in me, I allowed him to have a friend over to the house.

This was pure foolishness and desperation, . . . as if one five-year-old boy isn't enough for one house; two does not improve the situation. Well, I was congratulating myself for the wisdom of the decision, because the boys were playing so quietly. And then, too quietly.

I heard that sound that parents the world around dread: utter silence. I ran upstairs as fast as I could go and reached the hallway. I saw my son and his friend were kneeling in front of the linen closet. As I rounded the bend, my son had a great white box and from it he was lifting a baptismal gown that he had worn, that his father had worn, and that his grandfather before had worn on the days of their baptism.

As he held it aloft, my son turned to his friend and with great confidence said, "This is what I wore when I was hypnotized."

That's how we act, isn't it? Like we're hypnotizing them, putting them under some trance and we don't need to do another thing. We dedicate them, we baptize them. Maybe we hypnotize them a little. This will not do.

We act as though we put them under a trance from which they cannot escape. But baptism or dedication is not the end, it's the beginning. It says to the child, meet your family in Christ. Look around, these are the ones who by prayer and example will be there for you.

The Reformation and the Enlightenment, of course, heralded the coming of modernity. And there was nothing dearer to the heart of modernity and the last of the Reformation than the concept of rationality, the idea that God had true enough given us minds as a good gift.

The danger of the Reformation heritage is one of seeing children not as a real something but as a *potential* something. Seeing in them not who they are but who they will one day be. Now, that's a far piece from the fellow who said, Let those little children come to me and forbid them not, for of such is the Kingdom of God.

He didn't say, send them to the educational wing. When they're finished at Morehouse, send them back. Didn't say, cute baby. Take him some place for the next twenty-five years. He said, bring those children to me, bring them now. Bring them now.

The Reformation swung the pendulum too far in the direction of rationality. And the Church in the West largely concentrated its attentions on children's Christian education. We didn't let children minister to us and that was a mistake. That is always a mistake.

On the day the Challenger exploded, I had a son in nursery school. And I was busy in my office at work. The director of the nursery school at the Methodist church called and said, "Could you come? The children are so upset. We had put it on the television so that they could see. And, of course, it exploded. Would you come and talk with them?"

I said, "Of course I will." I was heartsick all the way from my office across the river to this nursery school, heartsick listening to the radio, heartsick thinking about the pride and dreams that died inside that space rocket. Heartsick. Thinking again, not for the first time, oh, Lord, my Lord. Why does this happen? Heartsick to have to go tell children this terrible news. I arrived and a couple of the boys were painting pictures, coloring pictures of rocket ships. My own son was among them. Andrew said to me as I arrived, "Mom, are those people in heaven?"

I said, "Yes, Andrew, I believe they are."

He responded, "I thought so, they were almost there."

I thought so. They were almost there. Me with my expensive education, snoot full of theological insight to share, a heartful of pastoral care. And the child says, "I thought so, Mom. They were almost there." A few hours later, the President of the United States made much the same point as he spoke of the astronauts touching the face of God.

So, we need to find the balance between education and spiritual formation. The balance between ministering to and ministering with children.

In all the many definitions that we have read of love, perhaps one of my favorites is the one that holds: to love is to know by heart the song another's heart sings and to hum it back to them on the days when they forget how it goes. Love is knowing the rhythm, the immutable rhythm of the heart. On those days, which we all have, when we forget how that tune goes, to just be there and hum back a few bars. Not suggest a countermelody or a new tempo—just hum it back until the familiar strains take hold again in the heart of the beloved.

It seems to me that on the macro scale, we need a chorus. We have a nation of bright hope and bold promise that all people are created equal, that there are certain inalienable rights, and that we hold these truths to be self-evident. Yet we've forgotten how the tune goes. We've forgotten its measures and melody, its rhythm. We've forgotten it is hard work. We've forgotten that it requires fair play.

The Church, it seems to me, should specialize in such humming. Our joyful duty should be helping each child discover the melody that lies within them.

One of the things the Black Church brings to this particular party, because of its own history and its own struggles, is that it has better retained children in the fullness of Church life. The Black Church didn't go so far in the direction of seeing children only as potentials. We need that gift again. We need to repristinate, to make pristine again, that Gospel: bring those children to me, forbid them not.

The Church needs to look across its long history. Yes, we did many good things. Public education in America began as a cottage industry of the Church. The abolition of child labor movement in America was led by a rabbi and two Christian ministers. Camps, conferences, children's choirs, sports teams, and Christian education in all its forms are grand contributions.

We have a strong tradition, but it's not nearly enough. The Church has collapsed to ideological forces that want to suggest that children belong alone to their parents and that the nuclear family somehow can be and should be the source of all support to the child. We must now acknowledge that that contradicts human history.

There is an ideology abroad in the land that says if a child suffers, it's the parents' fault. And if the parents can't make it, it's their problem. What is that, the Gospel turned on its head? Has the Church, or elements of it, not caved into such thought?

Our efforts to strengthen the family are laudable but those efforts cannot overcome the frailties of poor schools and deficient public policies. Our ministries with and to counseling families cannot act as if families are isolated from our societal contact. In our ministries with and counseling of families we cannot act as if families are isolated from societal contact. We cannot allow ourselves to concentrate only on the perfectability of the nuclear family.

Did the Scriptures say—and maybe I missed it— there came a nuclear family and offered their children to Jesus? No, they said it was a town where the children run together and they heard there was a famous rabbi in town. And so, as children do, all together those children came.

We can almost see the deacons, can't we, pushing them back, pushing them back, "This is an important man, step back children, you don't belong." Then the important man said, "Let them come here to me. Bring those children in here."

So, what time is it in the Church? I suggest to you that it is a time of disappointment and bitterness that must speak its name. With all the joyful and meaningful ministries with children, we must confess now those who have been left behind. Embracing the strengths of two thousand years of Church history we must acknowledge a need to discern anew, for this time and place, what the Lord requires of us as we minister to children in both the familial and societal contexts.

What time is it? It is time for fresh thinking both about our mission to children within the Church and those outside of it. It is time to review both our own callings and the nature of the society we live in today. Finally, it is time to act on the conviction that every child is the creation of a living God.

What Time Is It?
Time to Build a Sanctuary for Children Movement

We have just taken a whirlwind look at the place of children and child advocacy in the Church over more than 2,000 years. It brings us to the question of what time it is for the Church today. I believe it is time to affirm that this is the hour for freedom, the time for a Sanctuary for Children Movement.

As we consider what time it is for the Church today, let us listen for God's word to us in 1 Peter. And as we turn toward God's holy word, let us do so in prayer.

> Oh, God, open to us this day Your word, give us grace that we may open ourselves to You. Then by Your mighty grace open a portal into this world where we may live out Your word in faithfulness, truth, and mercy. So be it. Amen.

Listen then for God's word to us.

Rid yourselves, therefore, of all malice, and all guile, insincerity, envy, and all slander. [2]Like newborn infants, long for the

pure, spiritual milk, so that by it you may grow into salvation—³if indeed you have tasted that the Lord is good.
⁴Come to him, a living stone, though rejected by mortals yet chosen and precious in God's sight, and ⁵like living stones, let yourselves be built into a spiritual house, to be a holy priesthood, to offer spiritual sacrifices acceptable to God through Jesus Christ. ⁶For it stands in scripture: "See, I am laying in Zion a stone, a cornerstone chosen and precious; and whoever believes in him will not be put to shame." ⁷To you then who believe, he is precious; but for those who do not believe, "The stone that the builders rejected has become the very head of the corner," ⁸and "A stone that makes them stumble, and a rock that makes them fall." They stumble because they disobey the word, as they were destined to do.
⁹But you are a chosen race, a royal priesthood, a holy nation, God's own people, in order that you may proclaim the mighty acts of him who called you out of darkness into his marvelous light.
¹⁰Once you were not a people, but now you are God's people; once you had not received mercy, but now you have received mercy. (1 Peter 2:1–10)

Some years ago I read a newspaper commentary that made the point that in aeronautical navigation one fixes one's gaze upon the far horizon. To look at a point lower than the horizon is to land short of your goal, before you intend to. To look at a point above the horizon is never to land at all. Only if you fix your gaze just exactly at that far horizon do you bring the plane in safe and sound.

Where is the far horizon of the Church's vocation in child advocacy? As we look out across the distance and see the place where land and sky meet, what we do we see as the Church's ministry?— the witness to her risen Christ in the name of children?

I want to sketch a vision of that horizon as I now glimpse it. I'm like George Bernard Shaw, who said, I'm not a teacher, only a fellow traveler of whom you ask the way. I pointed ahead, ahead of myself as well as of you.

My mother has an adage for everything. Perhaps you were raised in the same gene pool. No matter what was happening, she had a saying. There's always a silver lining. Some days it's too wet to plow. She had an expression for everything. One of her admonitions to her children, when she didn't think they had adequate focus, was, If you don't know where you're going, any road will get you there. And that's my concern today.

We have been given this precious cornerstone, which the builders rejected. They said, away with him, we have no need of him. And in spite of it, he redeemed humanity. We have this precious cornerstone. The question in our hearts at this time is, what shall we build with it? Where are we going?

We're looking to the far horizon to see what edifice shall emerge for children. We have tried to formulate a theology of child advocacy. We have tried with open hearts and minds to look at Scripture and to be attentive in heart and mind to what Scripture calls us to do with children.

I want to suggest that that theology might be understood as "toward a sanctuary movement for children." I've never been in this building we're about to describe. I've never even absolutely seen it. But I believe I have dreamt it. I believe, more importantly, the prophets of old have dreamed of it. And I believe we have been given its cornerstone. So, let us go then and see if we can begin to describe among us what we would look like if we were a sanctuary movement for children.

It was not only the Children's Defense Fund's Samuel DeWitt Proctor Institute for Child Advocacy Ministry, where I have developed and delivered the substance of most of this book, that has made me think in this direction. Perhaps it was also the long saga of my own younger sister, born mentally retarded and physically handicapped, who never had Public Law 94/142, a program entitling her to education. It was a waste of time, they said in the 1950s and '60s. How dare they? The image of God is on her face as surely as on yours or mine. And somebody consigned her to a small future. The outrage of that decision perhaps has fueled my interest in children's advocacy. Through God's grace, my mother's good care, and her own courage, she is living a fulfilled life in her fifth decade, but she cannot thank our society.

Just as I was beginning ministry, I read *The Other America* by Michael Harrington. Do you remember that book? It came among us and told us of an America most of us didn't know existed or had only heard about but never seen. It told us a fifth of our people dwell there. *The Other America* was the source text for the war on poverty, the lofty idea that somehow in the intervening thirty years has transmutated into a war on the poor.

There was another text in those days that so influenced my thinking. It was a letter from a Birmingham jail. Did it not convict us, particularly the Church? Oh, said Dr. King, how very disappointed I am. Oh, how my heart breaks that the Church has been silent when it ought to speak and has spoken when it ought to be silent.

Even the stones would cry out. But the Church of Jesus Christ has kept its tongue. Well, in America, in this new millennium, it is time. It is the hour for freedom. We must do more. I say this with hope for a Church and nation that I love.

This will not be an individual undertaking. We have to covenant together with our churches—churches meaning both congregations and denominational structures, middle judicatories, and national denominations. We have to find a way.

The Other America and the letter from the Birmingham jail were modern epistles to the heart of the Church. And we haven't opened the letter yet. We have all but said "return to sender." We are not reading our mail.

It brings us back to the whole issue of human agency. We, we must work as the partners of God in the coming of a kingdom, or as I choose to say, kingdom, in which everybody gets the ticket stamped Yale. Nobody gets the ticket marked jail.

Today, in America, we are aging as the baby boom generation becomes, let's say, mature. There are three persons over age twelve for every child under twelve. There are nearly enough of us carry them one by one. Why can't we carry them all together? I believe because we haven't bound up our energies to one another in a functional way that allows us to exert an influence that's effective more than in a case by case basis. And that's why I ask us now to consider a sanctuary movement.

Often, as Charles West, Princeton theologian, says, we turn to God for help when our foundations are shaking only to find out it is God who's shaking them. Maybe it's for such a time as this that a place called Haley came into the ownership and husbandry of the Children's Defense Fund. How do we move from here?

I don't know all about the sanctuary movement, we'll have to discover that by God's grace as we move forward. But I know its essence. Its essence is that we must learn to see today with the eyes of tomorrow. We can't use our old vision.

Let's talk about the sanctuary movement. We need to watch our words because they become actions. We need to watch our actions because they become habits. Watch our habits, because they become character. And watch our character because it becomes destiny.

Why would I say sanctuary movement? Well, it sounds right, doesn't it? I mean, it has that nice kind of church ring to it. Sanctuary since the Middle Ages has been a concept attached to churches. We best see it in this country now in the work of those who took Central American and, sometimes, Mexican nationals into sanctuaries along the border, often in Texas and in California.

But sanctuary in the Middle Ages where the concept developed was the notion that one being chased by the police, the authorities, those in power, could run for a church, enter the domicile of the church, and not be forcibly removed for a period of time, usually forty days. During those days, during that sojourn or tenure inside the church, the church would use its good office to reconcile the issue at hand. When the asylum seeker reached the church or monastery he would ring the bell. Hence came the expression, "saved by the bell."

Where can our children run in America today? I don't mean just physically and geographically. Into whose arms may they go and say, my Lord, my Lord, I got the jail curriculum and I don't want to go? Where do they run to say, I'm hungry all the time. And I can't remember things. And I can't concentrate? Where do they go when violence overtakes them? What will it take for us to see that there must be both a sanctuary for children and a safe haven for childhood itself?

Where will it be safe to be a child, what will it take? Columbine, is that not enough of a wake-up call? Now, I know and I absolutely agree that guns are way too available. We need to get the guns out of the hands of, at least, young people. It would suit me fine if they were out of the hands of all of us. But certainly out of the hands of children.

I agree that parents today are too stressed and overburdened, perhaps too preoccupied, perhaps too ready to divorce and break up a family because they need fulfillment and are not giving enough concern for the ones they brought into the world. I agree with that.

I agree that there are psychological factors at work in young people who need medical attention and mental health care.

But I know a spiritual reality. Those issues just made it easier for the shooting to take place at Columbine. At the heart of Columbine, and I only use that one as an example, were some young men so alienated, so broken, so distanced from the community, so feeling alone that they decided in their tormented hearts that it was better to be wanted for murder than not to be wanted at all. They said, no one takes account of me. I will pay the price in order that they will heed me, that they will remember who I was. Drive people into a corner and they've got no way out except right straight over you.

In a time such as this, we as the Church must declare that it is the hour for freedom for our children. We must proclaim that the Church will be a sanctuary for children and make it so.

Why a sanctuary movement? Because the Church can't be just one more voice, weighing the expedience of this policy or that policy. We must be they who say children are our national treasure, our most valuable national resource. They aren't just our nation's treasure, they are God's treasure, and God will hold us accountable for how we are stewards of those children entrusted to us. And we, as an institution, will stand for them.

Sanctuary is not just bricks and mortar, though it's that, too. Let us not downplay the importance of physical space. Our world is a crowded world. It's not easy to find safe haven.

Sanctuary in its original notion, its Latin root, means the holy or consecrated place, that place where God can be encountered. That place where one may meet face to face the Holiest of Holies. Where in America can you go to face your God, to be given the peace to look upon the face of your God? The sanctum sanctorum concept of sanctuary.

The sanctuary movement is to my own thinking a form of piety and of spiritual discipline. Now, I want to be very careful here, because I'm not saying that we are to turn the Church into a totally child-centered organization. I hope I'm a better pastor than that. The Church has its own *raison d'être,* and its reason to be is to magnify the Lord, to celebrate the Christ who still lives, to worship and adore the everlasting God. So, I don't want to argue that the Church in its entirety should be child-centered. But I do believe that the Church has a particular vocation to get next to childhood and walk it home, to get right next to each child and see them into adulthood, the adulthood for which they were created.

There's also another notion of sanctuary that I alluded to, that notion of advocacy. A sanctuary doesn't just protect you from the powers outside, although sanctuary has always meant a place where the power struggle of the culture is realigned, where the powers outside and the power inside find some reconciliation that lets people live. Sanctuary also means standing with children as they find themselves in the world whether or not they are able to repair physically to the church itself.

Why sanctuary? Sanctuary as a concept continues the tradition of nonviolent change. It is a way to say we will have change, we will change the world, and we will do it by moral authority, no sticks, no bricks, no bats, no guns, no knives, no fists. By moral authority and the grace of God, we will see a new heaven and a new earth.

So much for why sanctuary. But why movement? Why do we talk about movement? After all, couldn't we just talk about a perspective? Well, I think there are some dimensions to movement that are absent in the child advocacy community today.

There is not a group of people who work on different aspects of child advocacy who have learned the importance of throwing their weight to each other's issues. Don't we jealously guard the juvenile justice crowd from the child-care crowd from the children's health crowd from the education crowd?

We're polite, of course. Yes, indeed, we're polite. Oh, that's all very, very interesting what you're doing. I'm going off to the health care caucus. Oh, you're doing that with the juvenile court, that's wonderful. Good-bye. I'm off to the education caucus.

Think of the freedom movement. Did they have a group that said we only desegregate water fountains? Sorry, my group does only lunch counters. I'd like to talk with you more about integration of the schools but I'm in the hotel discrimination caucus. No. It was a movement wise enough to know that any assault anywhere is a complete assault everywhere.

We have to find within ourselves the wisdom to know how and where to get the resources the movement for children needs. We need to build a movement and that's going to take an infrastructure. And the only friendly infrastructure I can think of is the Church.

I've been walking around this child advocacy vineyard for twenty-five years, trying to do the right thing, but never doing the hard, tedious work it's going to take to haul that cornerstone, given to us in Christ, and drag it to the far horizon and put it down, that stone rejected by the builders, and say on this rock we will build our church.

We will be AMEs and National Baptists, Presbyterians and Zen Buddhists for all I know. We're not trying to make a one-world church, we're not going to change our ways as regards our theology and worship tradition. But we're going to say we will identify ourselves as part of a movement, and through it we will express our oneness as regards children.

Imagine—are you seeing that far horizon?—imagine that place, scattered with churches. Inner-city churches in south central L.A., magnificent churches on the fancy avenues of Chicago and New York, suburban churches, and rural country prayer houses. Imagine if, in addition to the institutional sign that reads this is the First United Methodist Church or St. Mark's Episcopal, all of them have a sign that says "We are a sanctuary for God's children, all of them." All of them.

And that doesn't only mean children are safe here, though they are. It means, wherever children are unsafe, we go to them. The sanctuary is not an edifice entirely, it's also a spirit, a thought, a conviction.

Now, some of you will remember in the early 1970s there was a struggle for child-care licensing and regulation. Many of us took a real bruising in that battle. We worked very hard and we had a wonderful bill passed in 1971. Then it came to President Nixon's desk and at the urging of those who opposed mothers in the workforce, President Nixon vetoed the bill calling it the broadest plan yet advanced for the Sovietization of American children. Talk about hyperbole!

I never did follow that reasoning. But it was effective. Those of us on the other side of the battle were labeled the Kiddie Liberation Movement. We would hear about ourselves on television and in newspapers, being accused, "If they get their way, children will have the right to sue their parents."

It was no such thing. We were looking to WIC, the Special Supplemental Food Program for Women, Infants, and Children, and Title 20, and food stamps not as a substitute for parental care but as a tool that parents used in their own good parenting of their children. We were supporting, not supplanting, the parents.

We need to do this, create a sanctuary for children movement. Dr. Otis Moss Jr. once remarked that we sometimes lament some misdeed that we've done. But our sorrow for that which we have left undone is inconsolable when we did not respond to the convictions of our heart.

So, I ask you this day, are you convicted in your heart that we must find another way? We must find a way with one another and with our congregations and across this land. We must find ways to put wheels, as they say, under a movement for children within the churches.

My friends at All Saints Episcopal Church in Pasadena have been helpful in the development of thinking about a sanctuary for children movement. All Saints is a sanctuary for children church and there are three or four other very splendid examples, each expressing it in their own way.

They bring to mind the bird sanctuary. In a bird sanctuary, the people running the bird sanctuary don't become the mother and father birds. They're not out there giving flying lessons. They only create a place that's safe enough for the mother birds and the father birds to teach the flying lessons. We're not going to adopt all of America's children and raise them our way. We're going to make a safe place where their mamas and daddies can teach their baby birds how to fly.

We have many philosophers to whom we turn. One of my favorites is Charles Schultz, creator of *Peanuts*. He says, Life is like a ten-speed bicycle; most folks have more gears than they've ever used. I think it's true of the Church. The Church has some gears that need some loosening up. We can no longer be satisfied, as important as it is, just to focus on Christian education for our children. As important as it is, our Head Start or our free school or after-school program is not enough.

It is time. We have to declare ourselves. For the life of the world, we need desperately a sanctuary for children movement.

I believe in the sanctuary movement, and you know that a *belief* is distinct from an idea. A belief is not merely an idea the mind possesses. A belief is an idea that possesses the mind. We must move toward that far horizon, strengthened by our belief. And then we can proclaim and claim the scripture: Once we were no people, but now we are God's people. Once there was no safe place. And now there is a sanctuary.

What will be the program of such a sanctuary movement, I don't know. But I know this, that by God's grace in God's good time it shall be given unto us.

CHAPTER SIX

What Just Happened?
What Must Happen for Children to Catch Our Dreams

Finally, we must ask, What just happened? and take a hard look at the context in which our children live and die, thrive and suffer, hope and despair. It is time for us as a Church, as a nation, and as a world to stop misleading each other and answering, nothing! when asked what just happened, when asked what has happened to our children today.

I'm sorry to tell you what you already know, the context is Babylon. And Psalms says, *"By the rivers of Babylon—there we sat down and there we wept when we remembered Zion. On the willows there we hung up our harps. For there our captors asked us for songs, and our tormentors asked for mirth, saying, 'Sing us one of the songs of Zion! How could we sing the* LORD'*s song in a foreign land?"* (Psalm 137:1–4).

Sing we will of freedom. Scholars of African American hymnody have often told us that, like so much in that rich tradition, the hymnody of the African American community in this country sings and teaches with an ambiguity, with a certain mystery inherent in it. In the earliest records a well-known hymn was sung "Oh, Freedom, oh freedom, oh freedom over me, before I was a slave I *was* buried in my grave. I went home to my Lord, *now* I'm free." There is embedded in that song an ambiguity that speaks of the truth. Here is captured the truth of dignity and determination—even within the context of the inhumanity of slavery. In Babylon we may sing to freedom.

We turn now to the context into which the Church must speak. I believe we live in a myopic age, an age in which the vision is not so clear and what vision there is, is horribly nearsighted. Well, what does the prophet Habakkuk say to us about this matter of vision?

In Habakkuk, you remember the prophet Habakkuk, we hear the lament, Oh, Lord how long must I wait? When will you answer my supplications? When, oh, Lord, will you let me see? When are you going to restore my vision? (From chapter 1, paraphrased). When are you going to do one of those operations they do today that's going to let me see?

And while Habakkuk is complaining and wailing, the voice of the Lord comes and says, Now. Wait on your watch post. Watch post. Stand at your watch post and then you write the vision large, very large so that even the runner going past can read it (Habakkuk 2:1–2, paraphrased).

Even the runner. Even the busy harried executive on his way to his second million. Even the soccer mom who has three more car-pools can catch a glimpse. Write the vision large. Don't make it complicated and, for heaven sakes, don't make any fine print. We live in a myopic time. An era of nearsightedness and short arms. So write the vision large, says the prophet. And what shall we write?

The Children's Defense Fund tells us the statistical story of what just happened to children in America and it's a grim picture. Now, every year CDF comes out with *The State of America's Children* and I can't decide whether to read it each year or not. I keep hoping that I'm going to open it up and somehow the numbers are going to jump around and it's going to say most of our children are well. It's going to say they're all getting their inoculations; it's going to say they're all in safe places. But every year I open it up, and oh, there may be improvement here or there, but as one of my children would say, it's a car wreck. It's a plain car wreck.

And then we read in our newspaper, even if we ignore the research, our children are killing children. In Jonesboro. There's a disease of children with guns slaughtering children in their schools. Billy gunned down his teacher last Tuesday. And Simon wiped out his reading class in April. And some fool stood up and said well, we shouldn't change the gun laws, that's not the problem.

In the *New York Times,* you know, all the news that's fit to print, someone with a long title and a fat salary said, "It is thought perhaps the easy access to guns may be part of the problem." It is thought that PERHAPS that easy access to guns *might* be part of the problem?

Dr. Samuel DeWitt Proctor once spoke of a terrible day as a child when he joined other children in name-calling a woman who was lowly, hurt, and despised. What's worse, it's not just boys who have to prove their sovereignty, to show that they can be bad on demand, as Sam Proctor said, but our government has joined the chorus and said it's fine to call them "Crazy Ida," add to the burden, give them the guns. Don't regulate anything because this is the price of freedom. Nonsense, nonsense.

Periodically, a study of children and their own hopes and prospects is released and enables us to see what children believe about their lives. For some years, I've been astonished to read that a majority of our children do not believe they will grow to an old age. Two-thirds, two out of three, believe they will not live a long life. And what do they think is going to take them? The list of horrors includes (1) they believe a random act of violence will cut them down, (2) they believe an act of violence in their home will take them, (3) they believe an act of violence in school will take them, (4) they believe the environment will poison them with noxious air and an absence of water, and (5) they believe a virus, perhaps yet unknown, will wipe them out in an epidemic. A pandemic we would say.

Two-thirds of our children don't believe they will live to an old age. Now if there is a threat to freedom, I suggest that's it. A generation that doesn't believe it has any life to live for, a generation that's lost sight of the possibility of a life fulfilled, is a dangerous generation. Beloved, "Foxes have holes, and birds of the air have nests; but the Son of Man has nowhere to lay his head" (Luke 9:58). How can we face that these feelings in our children have grown up among us?

Some years ago, I had some seminarians who were in for the summer, working in my office, do a study of children. I was curious to know what children thought their pastoral care needs were. Now, you don't ask children, what are your pastoral needs? We asked them the question in this way. We said, "What are the days you think the pastor ought to be there for you?" So, I sent these students out and they came back with a most interesting set of answers. The number one pastoral need the children noted for themselves, the day they thought the pastor ought to be there for them, the number one answer, was when the pets die.

When their pets die, when their parents die or divorce, when they get left back, when their best friend leaves. With those answers, we asked pastors, "What do you think are the important moments for the church in its ministry to children?" And rather predictably, they said baptism or dedication, confirmation, graduation, wedding. This is what we refer to as being on parallel planes of conversation.

These two trajectories never meet. I'm in agony because I got left back, and you're planning my confirmation class. I'm scared to go to school, to walk the streets, to go home—and you're planning for Youth Sunday. Now there's nothing wrong with Youth Sunday or confirmation or baptism or dedication. They're all necessary and important ministries of the Church. But they don't deal with our children's fears. They don't touch their broken hearts. They don't make children whole.

When one of my sons was young, his father was engaged in a program that took him to Russia once every six weeks. And our boy was little and used to drive with his father and me down to the airport in Newark. In Newark there's an observation deck; we'd drop off Daddy and we'd go up to the observation deck so that we could wave good-bye to Daddy's plane. Now with the interval that it takes to wait for an international flight, we didn't always wait for the exact right plane. This was a deception to shorten a long wait. (Look, there was a plane and there was a daddy on it, I feel sure. This is a deception being shared among parents, I think.)

So, we stood on top of the observation deck and we would watch and wave and wave, bye daddy, bye daddy, bye daddy. The plane would take off and circle around Manhattan and then head back south, and we would wave and wave and wave until it got so small we couldn't see it anymore.

Some months later we were leaving on a family vacation. We boarded our plane and this same boy was sitting over near the window, head down, hands clinched. I thought it was wonderful that the child was praying, a child saying his prayers. This went on for some time. Finally, I asked, "Andrew, are you all right?"

He said, "Mom, when do we get small?" Children have fears we don't begin to understand. Imagine you're three years old and now you're in a plane and you've seen with your own eyes what happens.

Well, as you know, I was in theology not science so I don't really know why it works that way. So I just told him, "Andrew, when you're in the plane, it's the ground that gets small. And I don't quite know why it works that way."

We have to find a way to take seriously our children's fears. Whatever their fears may be, we must find it within ourselves to address them.

Why is it so? Why is America such a fearful place for our children? Why are they dying? Why are they born small? Why don't they ever get a chance? Why do we give up on them? Why do we forget them?

I want to suggest that America stands today at the latter end of a long, historical trajectory in which children have moved from an economic asset to an economic liability. Children have moved from a national resource to a national problem. Children have moved from the blessed, beloved in God's own image to children who are perceived as threatening strangers to us.

In America, we are victims of a kind of cruel social Darwinism. You know, the idea that the race goes to the swift. Never mind measuring where the starting line was, never mind making provision for those who started further back. Not on the track, not in the stadium even, not even on the flat, but over the other side of the hill. At the signal "go," obstacles were put before them. We only measure when they come across that last line. Not how they got there, not what courage it took. The ones that streak, reeking of entitlement, we celebrate. Those who come limping in, having made it over the mountains, over the hills, under the wall, through the flames, between the gunshots, by the time they cross the finish line, we've gone home. We've turned out the stadium lights. The ribbons and medals are long since gone. No ribbons, no medals. You know, we don't much care whether they finish at all. In fact, we've been known to take up the track. We've been known to make it into a shopping mall before they could even enter the race.

So, this ugly social Darwinism that lies in contradiction to everything we know to be true portrays the devolution of a society that has now lost sight of its own beliefs. I love this land. I know its problems but I love this land. I was seduced. I was seduced by the songs of my youth, "Oh beautiful for heroes was proved in liberating strife. Who more than self their country loved and mercy more than life. America, America, God mend thine every flaw. Confirm her soul in self-control, in liberty and law." And I believed it. I thought it true. And I believe it still, and we will sing that song no matter what our tormentors require of us.

America has lost her connection with her own dreams and high purposes. We live in a society, a postmodern society, that's itemized: get yours, get your family's, get your own. Don't ask, what is in the common good, but what is in my good.

For many years I worked in central and Eastern Europe from time to time. My translator was a wonderful woman named Olga. Olga was a believer when it was dangerous to be a believer. She would ask me as we walked in the streets—never when we were in the hotels or the meeting rooms—but as we walked along in some safe space, she would ask me to pray with her or to read to her a Psalm.

Well, a different day has come to Olga's land. I saw her a few years ago after the fall of the old Soviet Union, and once again we walked in the park because it had become our habit to walk and talk only outside. I said to her, "Olga, are you happy? Does your hope soar?"

To my great surprise she said, "Well, sort of. I'm glad for the freedom, I'm glad for the Church and its rebirth. But the coming of the free market economy scares me because I don't know whether there can be a free market economy without cultural decadence. Because anything that can be sold will be sold and to whomever controls the currency to buy it."

I thought to myself, Olga, my friend, is right. The jury is still out on that question. Can there be a free market economy without cultural decadence? This is a very serious question for our America. Our society too often seems resigned to a kind of perpetual anger. It can't even remember what it was mad at or why it's mad. It just remembers to draw the circle close and to castigate those who stand outside of it.

We come from different parts of America but I know one thing sure, wherever you live, there's a little bit of Egypt there. Wherever you are, there's a little enslavement there. Wherever we live, we've got to shake the dust of that land off our feet and head for the land that is promised to us.

Everything is at stake in America today. In the way of the world, America is in her adolescence. We're not a very old country. We're in our adolescence. You remember adolescence? Long legs, big feet. Pimples, uncertainty, fear, and concern. And we have it all. We're gangling, loping youth in the midst of the community of the world's nations. But we're a bold and big and powerful youth and we can intimidate. Sometimes we all need a tap on the shoulder, and sometimes

America needs a tap on the shoulder. But who's to give it? But who's to give it? We just barge around in our youthful way, making judgments one on top of the other and no one to turn us aside.

What are we to do? I don't know, but here are some suggestions, just some suggestions. First, I believe, we need to recognize that freedom is as we proclaimed, an inalienable right. It doesn't come from a correct political perspective or an effective political strategy. Freedom is the intended destiny of every human. Freedom is an inalienable right. Mahatma Gandhi said, just a few days before he was gunned down, "I implore you all to stop your insane actions at once. Let not future generations say that you lost the sweet bread of freedom because you could not digest it."[1]

Let me say that again. Gandhi said, "Stop your insane actions. Let not future generations say you lost the sweet bread of freedom because you could not digest it." Let it not be said of us. We have to recognize and reclaim this inalienable right. We need to learn anew how to digest the bread of freedom. In a special way, that bread of freedom has to be extended to each new generation. This is the task of a children's movement.

We have to have a children's movement. We cannot just have a friendship club that celebrates other good folks who do something for children. We must become more strategic, better disciplined, able to set priorities and commit ourselves to walking hand-in-hand, step-by-step together in a movement.

We have to learn to throw our weight for each other's issues, which means that we're going to have to learn more about each other's issues. You're in child care. Well, friend, you're also in violence prevention; you're also in gang ministry; you're in public education. We have to celebrate the leadership that is among us, and we have plenty. We have to fall in behind leadership on each issue.

In America today there are real and frightening threats to our children, and there are many strategies to address the various challenges. One of the most persistent problems is the bullying that children and families feel on the part of the governmental agencies that find fault and threaten those they are to help. Faced with decades of official bullying, families and child advocates are tempted to say that Goliath is too big. We need among us the heart of David, who said that Goliath is too big to miss! The shepherd David then went after the bully and triumphed over him.

Too big to miss, too deadly to miss, too mean to miss. There are Goliaths rampaging around the country. We have to fall in together as a movement. Think of Mahatma Gandhi when he urged us not to be afraid. "We in India may in a moment realize that 100,000 Englishmen need not frighten 300 million human beings."[2] We must in a moment realize that a 100,000 Englishmen cannot scare us. Then how can less than 600 in the Congress put fear into us? Don't we know our numbers?

I want to suggest just these initial directions, that we identify our allies, close ranks, learn to work together, and get behind the Davids. The Davids are those brave and resourceful few like Marian Wright Edelman who bring clarity and leadership. Then as the people of God it is my utter and profound belief that what the Church brings to the party of the children's movement is the history, tradition, and practice of a sanctuary movement. Let us declare that it will no longer be said in our America that the children were left to fend for themselves. Let it be said of us that we created safe space, physical safe space, cultural safe space. That we were the adults who said no. No to violent toys, no to lawlessness on the Internet that makes children the object of adult entertainment. Let it be said of us that we're the people who said no to cereal companies that pander cereal that the children would be better off if they ate the box it came in. Let it not be said that it's okay and even profitable to think of the next most violent video game.

Let us study the ways of nonviolence ourselves. Let us look again at Gandhi and at King and Mrs. Rosa Parks. We must study again the ways of nonviolence. Train ourselves, teach ourselves, discipline ourselves, hold ourselves to the commitment of nonviolence.

Think of Archbishop Desmond Tutu at the end of apartheid rule and the beginning of South African freedom. He said, the struggle had not been for a black-ruled South Africa but rather for something far more difficult, for a South Africa governed by Blacks and Whites and Coloreds" (as the distinction is in South Africa). We haven't asked too much of our people, said Tutu. We have asked too little. It's not that our dream, our vision in a myopic world, has been too large. It is that it has been so miniscule. We need a big vision, an encompassing vision, a vision that is whole. And so with that, the anti-apartheid movement began to talk about a mixed-race governing South Africa. Now in those days, you know, that was a logical null set. A mixed-raced South Africa? What is that? A camel who flies?

The vision was whole. Desmond Tutu has often made the point: There is absolutely nothing you can do to make God love you more. God already loves you. Your job is to show the love of God which is in Jesus Christ to a weary world. Here we dare suggest that it might be the world of children.

When one of my sons was about three, I was lifeguarding at the backyard swimming pool. You know, one of those little round pools a few inches deep where after the first five minutes, there are more grass clippings than there are children and water. As they played on this hot day, my son grew thirsty. I was sitting in my lifeguard lawn chair having a lemonade. My little son came up to me to ask for a sip, and I stretched out the lemonade glass to him. Just as he took it toward his lips, you almost could see his nursery school teacher loom up in his mind, the specter of a lecture on preschool hygiene. He stopped and asked, "If I drink from this, will I catch your dreams?" Now he meant germs but had gotten his words mixed up. "Will I catch your dreams?" He drank the lemonade and went back. And I sat there and I thought, oh my son, if all it took for you to know my dreams for you; if all it took was for us to sip a little lemonade from a common glass, then you would know what I hold in my heart for your life. You would see yourself as I see you at your little age and your hopes would soar. But, of course, it was just a slip of the tongue.

And then I thought of a man who said, I have a dream. And I thought of another man who said, Take, drink. This is my cup. All of you drink from it. And like I so often do, I learn my theology at the feet of my children, one of whom said, If I drink of your cup, will I catch your dreams? And I wonder now, if that's not what Jesus had in mind. Take, drink from this cup, and glimpse my dream for humanity. Drink all of you of this cup and drink deeply and catch the dream of a world made whole. Of a peaceable kingdom living in love and justice. Of a Church that is worthy of the calling to which it is called: to be the body of Christ. Pray God that we catch that dream. AMEN and AMEN!

Notes

1. Mahatma Gandhi, "Riots and Independence," *The Way to Communal Harmony*, www.mahatma.org.in/books.
2. Mahatma Gandhi, "The Doctrine of the Sword," www.salsa.net/peace.